E

M000118675

The further we go in God, the less we can take with us. It's His love and kindness that requires this level of surrender. For us to possess the promises He has for us, we must first learn to value His Presence above all things. Without this gift, the promise just won't satisfy. Lana Vawser has written a tremendous book on the new season that is upon us as the Church. *I Hear the Lord Say, "New Era"* beautifully challenges and prepares us for what the Lord longs to pour out in this next move of His Spirit, but it will not come without a fresh sacrifice on our part.

Lana writes with purity and a prophetic passion that implores believers to seek His face above all else. Her words realign our hearts to the priority of the one thing: *Jesus*. This book carries such a timely message, but more importantly, a timely impartation for the Body of Christ. Our pursuit of Him will cost us, yes, but it's this wonderful friendship with Him that becomes our greatest adventure and reveals the purpose for which we were born.

BILL JOHNSON
Bethel Church, Redding, CA
Author of *The Way of Life* and *Raising Giant-Killers*

I believe that there is a new era coming to the body of Christ, and the Church is going to look very different from how it looks now. God is preparing His children to be ready for the biggest harvest the world has ever seen. I love Lana Vawser's new book, *I Hear the Lord Say "New Era."* Through a dream encounter, the Lord has revealed to Lana strategic ways to position ourselves with God in order to walk the way Jesus walked (see 1 John 2:6). This book really witnessed to me because I myself have had a similar encounter of a new era rising up in the Spirit and the power of Elijah!

Thank you, Lana, for your obedience in writing this treasure as an invitation for believers.

ADAM F. THOMPSON
Prophetic minister and international author
www.voiceoffireministries.org

What can I say? Let it be known to the reader that what you hold in your hands right now is pure gold, a treasure from heaven to the body of Christ for this hour we are in.

I Hear the Lord Say "New Era" is a bold clarion call that has been forged in the fire of intimacy. Truly, this message is a gift from the Father's heart to His dear beloved, revealing insight and understanding into the blueprints of heaven as we launch forward into this new era. The pages of this book deeply challenge, align, encourage, and speak into our walk with the Lord, equipping us to walk a victorious path in these days ahead. The Lord says in Amos 3:7 that He does nothing in the earth without revealing it to His prophets first. Lana is a true prophet who walks closely with the Lord, intensely, and intentionally. Her heart and walk with the Lord exemplify the picture of Mary of Bethany who was praised by the Lord for choosing the "better portion" of sitting at His feet and listening to His words (see Luke 10:42). The Lord's presence is Lana's portion; thus, the content of a book of this kind undeniably resounds the frequencies of heaven for His people in this season. He who has ears to hear, hear what the Spirit of the Lord is saying to the Church.

ANITA ALEXANDER
Revival Flame Ministries
Gold Coast, Queensland, Australia
www.revival-flame.org

If you could sit at the feet of God with a journal ready in hand and ask, "God, what are the keys for this next era? What will help prepare me and the people for what You are about to do?"—that's what you have in your hand. I have no doubt that as you read these words that my dear friend Lana Vawser has knit together in her beautiful book you will find confirmation for your life that you are right in step with what God is doing and saying; you will find encouragement in these keys and also proper and right alignment for what's coming. As Lana would say, "The best is yet to come!" Be encouraged. You get to play a part in one of the most exciting times to be alive in history!

ANA WERNER
Founder of Ana Werner Ministries
President, Eagles Network
Author of *The Seer's Path, Seeing Behind the Veil, The Warrior's Dance*
Co-author of *Accessing the Greater Glory*
www.anawerner.org

Once again, Lana has produced a book "for such a time as this." There is so much of the Father's heart in this book for the new era that we are in. This will be a book that is read and reread by people who know that Jesus' Kingdom is here with us and working through us. Within these pages you will discover real and tangible prophetic words that are ushering in the new era.

MATT BECKENHAM
Pastor, Haberfield Baptist Church

In this book Lana clearly communicates the Father's tone of urgency and the great divide that is now upon us. In these pages is a clarion release for the emerging Ekklesia to shift into the new day and be first responders to His voice. As you read Lana's words, I believe the doubled-edged sword of His Word is going to forge and commission a generation of fiery messengers who will be rooted in righteousness and truth. May we be found upright in the way of His judgments and may the inhabitants of the world see the beauty of His righteousness!

TOM LEDBETTER
Founding Elder of East Gate Community Church
Founder and Director of Kingdom Gravity Ministries
Founder and Director of the School of Dream Intelligence

Lana Vawser's *I Hear the Lord Say "New Era"* is one of the most insightful and relevant books of our time. We are clearly living in one of the greatest seasons in history, as God is releasing an extraordinary shift in the earth. The very manifest glory of the Lord is about to consume the nations on an unparalleled scale in the fulfillment of ancient prophecy. As I read this powerful manuscript, I was profoundly stirred that this is a must-read for all those whose lives are completely devoted to Jesus and who desire to be ready for this awe-inspiring move of glory. There is an urgency in this hour for us to fully prepare ourselves in purity as the Bride of Christ and to fulfill our God-given mandate as mature believers ready for the great harvest. Jesus is coming to cleanse and empower His "called-out ones," the *Ekklesia*. *I Hear the Lord Say "New Era"* will give you the strategic insight and wisdom you need to walk in greater intimacy and power with God. You will glean powerful truths from Lana's years of abiding in the secret place and from her life-changing revelatory encounters. I have had the great honor of walking with Lana for many years as a friend and as a spiritual father in the faith. I believe that as you read her labor of love, you are going to receive an extraordinary impartation from Lana Vawser's life that will help prepare you to walk out all that God has for you in this greatest move of glory.

GARY BEATON
Founder and president of Transformation Glory International
Author, speaker, and prophetic voice to the nations
transformationglory.com

I Hear the Lord Say "New Era" carries fire! Its pages are alive and speak deep to the very core of our hearts and what God is doing in this time. My insides didn't just resonate with every word but came to attention as if a trumpet was blasting a decree! This is a *kairos* road map for the extraordinary era we have entered, filled with wisdom, prophetic insight, and spiritual discernment that thunders off the pages. Such *kairos* words can only come from one who has lingered in the presence of God long enough to be a trusted friend who hears His secrets. Lana Vawser is such a friend of God, and from her pen tangible anointing is imparted, as is clarity, peace, and an urgency of personal recalibration to uncompromising service of the King. This isn't just a book; it's an announcement from heaven. I can't recommend it to you enough! Your insides will burn, and you will know, "I have heard the heart of my King Jesus" in these pages.

JODIE HUGHES
Pour It Out Ministries
Author, *The King's Decree*
www.pouritout.org

This is a profoundly rich and powerful book that really rings true as the word of the Lord for this season. May His words through Lana help you embrace and prepare for this exciting new era.

KATHERINE RUONALA
Senior Leader, Glory City Church, Brisbane
Founder and facilitator of the Australian Prophetic Council

What you hold in your hand is an invitation into the depths of the Father's heart for the new era that is upon us. You will find yourself equipped with keys, divine strategy, and prophetic insight to navigate this new era. You will feel your heart provoked to deeper hunger for Jesus and greater intimacy in the chambers of God's holy presence. With every word of her new book, my beautiful friend Lana writes a love note to Jesus. He is truly glorified on every page, which, as Lana states in this book, is essential in this new era—"Eyes fixed on Jesus." As a result, when you read you will be gripped by the truth dripping from every page. This book is a strategic guide for the body of Christ as we run full speed ahead into all God has for us. A must-read for us all as we advance the Kingdom and shine bright the light of Jesus in our everyday lives.

KRISSY NELSON
Author, speaker, and TV host
Krissy Nelson Ministries

The Holy Spirit will confirm His word by two and three witnesses or testimonies. What is interesting is that very phrase is used in three different key places in the Word of God itself. One of the words I have been carrying for months is that we are not just entering into a new day, a new year, or even a new decade, but rather an entire new era in the body and Christ and the world around us. Lana Vawser from Australia is one of those next-generation voices in the global prophetic movement who has emerged as a voice of accuracy, content, and credibility. This book you hold in your hand is one that I really love. Why? Lana Vawser has brought a fresh perspective to the days we live in, including a gaze into where we are going. Isn't that what prophets are supposed to do? Thanks, Lana, for being such a clear voice in this strategic hour.

JAMES W. GOLL
Founder of God Encounters Ministries and GOLL Ideation LLC
Bestselling author, consultant, and communications coach

The revelation being released regarding this new era is unprecedented. Lana has written an excellent book to inform and inspire us to press on and move forward into the greatest days of church history. The *Ekklesia* needs these foundational keys in this season. Read it, study it, pray and release it, and be encouraged.

DR. TIM SHEETS
Pastor, Oasis Church
Bestselling author of *Angel Armies* and *The New Era of Glory*

These pages before you hold some of the greatest keys to navigate this new era that we as the Church have entered into. Lana's deep and pure heart is laid bare as she passionately implores every willing ear to hear, eye to see, and heart to perceive the great invitation that Jesus is calling us into at this time. These words possess power to re-ignite lukewarm hearts, and to release the faithful further into the heights of God's great plans for this moment in time. This book is the very heart of God for His beautiful children to be gracefully awoken and purposefully activated to arise in purity, maturity, humility, and holiness, for such a time as this. It is truly my honor to recommend my friend, Lana Vawser, and this awe-inspiring message for this very hour.

NATALIE FULLER
Author of *Positioned for Purpose*
nataliefuller.co

Friends—true friends—of God are those positioned to most effectively discern how He is moving and what He is doing. They can trace the times and seasons of the Holy Spirit with great accuracy and integrity. Why? They know His nature, they love Him, and even above their own wants and longings, they desire to see their Father's plans and purposes come to pass in the earth.

People across the earth have been blessed by the powerful ministry of Prophet Lana Vawser. Her words, insights, and prophecies carry weight because she has never graduated from friendship with God. Period. That's the secret to recognizing new spiritual seasons and yes, even announcing new eras—ever keeping one's head resting upon the chest of Jesus. Lana has delivered a gift to the body of Christ with *I Hear the Lord Saying "New Era!"* But get ready! The words in this book are like holy fire igniting you to take your unique place in this pivotal moment in history. It's not a new day or a new season; it's a New Era, and that means everything is changing!

LARRY SPARKS, MDIV.
Publisher, Destiny Image
larrysparksministries.com
Author of *Breakthrough Faith, Ask for the Rain* and
Accessing the Greater Glory
Host of *The Prophetic Edge*

I HEAR
THE LORD SAY

New Era

DESTINY IMAGE BOOKS BY LANA VAWSER

The Prophetic Voice of God

A Time to Selah

I HEAR
THE LORD SAY

New Era

BE PREPARED, POSITIONED,
AND PROPELLED INTO
GOD'S PROPHETIC
TIMELINE

LANA VAWSER

DESTINY IMAGE® PUBLISHERS, INC.

P.O. Box 310, Shippensburg, PA 17257-0310

"Promoting Inspired Lives."

This book and all other Destiny Image and Destiny Image Fiction books are available at Christian bookstores and distributors worldwide.

Cover design by Eileen Rockwell

Interior design by Terry Clifton

For more information on foreign distributors, call 717-532-3040.

Reach us on the Internet: www.destinyimage.com.

ISBN 13 TP: 978-0-7684-5415-4

ISBN 13 eBook: 978-0-7684-5416-1

ISBN 13 HC: 978-0-7684-5418-5

ISBN 13 LP: 978-0-7684-5417-8

For Worldwide Distribution, Printed in the U.S.A.

1 2 3 4 5 6 7 8 / 24 23 22 21 20

DEDICATION

Jesus, this is for you! For your Glory! Thank You for the invitation to pen what's on Your heart. I am forever thankful. To be invited into a place of knowing You, hearing Your voice, seeing You and making You known in the earth—there is no greater privilege and I am forever thankful!

CONTENTS

FOREWORD

When Lana Vawser asked me to write the foreword for *I Hear the Lord Say "New Era,"* my heart leapt. This book is for today! We are living in a crisis: physical, economic, political, and spiritual. We must remain filled with faith as we journey into this era ahead. Recently, I saw a dress and knew it was for my daughter, Rebekah, who is a writer in Hollywood. This dress reminded her of all her dreams for the future. After she received this gift, she wrote the following:

> We're in a moment and it feels endless. Like
> we've touched the edge of a black hole and time
> is warped, slowed down and maybe even broken.

Don't lose sight of your hope in the future. Never stop being the little girl (or boy) playing dress up when the whole world tells you it's silly. Never stop dreaming, and most importantly, don't stop doing everything you can to break through.

We have entered a new era where the impossible will become the norm! There is a moment when time makes a shift and you gain momentum for your future. We are in that Kingdom moment now. We have not just entered a new year, decade, or season, but a new era in the Kingdom of God.

In Isaiah 32:1, the Word of God says, «*Look—a new* **era** *begins! A king will reign in righteousness, and his princes according to justice!*" (TPT). An era is a fixed point in time from which a series of years is reckoned. An era can also be a memorable or important date or event in the history of a thing, person, or nation. An era is a system of chronological notation computed from a given date as a basis. An era is a period identified by some prominent figure or characteristic feature or stage in development. *We have entered a new Kingdom era.* In Hebrew this era is known as *Pey,* which means voice or mouth. As God's ambassadors, our voices must be heard this decade. ***We will decree a thing and it will happen!***

We are entering a season when we decree our future! The words of our mouth are very key. This book is a guide for how to decree your future and establish the presence of God around you. We are living in an Upper Room season and Lana thoroughly details the call to the Upper Room.

Without a vision, a people perish. In Proverbs 29:18, this word actually means that without boundaries or prophetic utterance a people go backward. *We are moving from a* **Church** *era to a* **Kingdom** *era.*

In this divine shift, the Lord is transforming our mindset so we move outwardly from what has been built in one season, into a new movement for the next season. This will be a new building season, but first we must unlock God's Kingdom plan and align heaven and earth.

The Spirit of God is now imparting to leadership to establish an incredible, indestructible blueprint for the future. Lana discusses the power that it takes to enter in to this era. She reminds us of key leaders that moved in Holy Spirit and then exhorts us that the Church will tremble again as it moves forward into this new historic time.

This book, *I Hear the Lord Say "New Era,"* will prepare you for the season ahead. Lana addresses the conflicting and conflicted times that are creating our choices in the midst of this war season. We are meant to cross over into prosperity, but we choose to have our way in a situation, instead of submitting to the will of God. We are in a great warfare over a threefold cord controlled by Satan's kingdom consisting of poverty, infirmity and religion.

We are heading to what is known as a new normal, and into a decade of deliverance. This book invites you to learn how to step into a new fiery river that will cause your faith to explode. Relish every word that is here as heaven and earth realign around you with the revelation that is shared in these pages.

DR. CHUCK D. PIERCE
President, Global Spheres, Inc.
President, Glory of Zion International Ministries

FOREWORD

I love the prophetic! This beautiful gift helps us to navigate well during times of transition. Knowing the will, ways, and word of the Lord is essential for living a fruitful life before Him.

Months prior to 2020, numbers of credible prophets foresaw a new era emerging and very soon into the new year, signs of that new era were glaring at all on a global level. Beginning with a viral pandemic, economic shakings and racial tensions, the masses were unsettled, fearful, and deeply concerned on many levels. Many questions and insecurities surfaced, and everyone was talking about the "new normal". What is this new normal? In this season, what is God wanting to see in

His church...in the world? Lana Vawser will reveal many answers to these question in her book, *I Hear the Lord Say "New Era!"*.

An era is more than just a new year, season, or decade. It is a long and distinct period of history with unique features and characteristics. With this in mind, it is important that we are rightly positioned as we enter into this new period of mankind's history. This era will be an era of distinct change and reform. We will see God at work to establish His purposes, and it is vital in these extreme days to draw close to Him and align with His Word.

I have prayed with and for Lana as she was receiving many of the prophetic words you will find in the following pages. Often, she would be in deep travail and wrestlings of her soul as she was receiving and giving birth to the revelation you will read in this book. Lana Vawser prophesies words from the heart of God that will not only impact you, but will align and transform you if you heed their instruction. Lana understands the emotion of God as well as the purpose of God and she has in the fear of the Lord, carefully stewarded the prophetic insights contained in this book so that they will settle, build, strengthen, and establish you.

I Hear the Lord Say "New Era!" will open your eyes to great invitations from the Lord for you. Put your trust in the Lord your God and you will be established. Put your trust in His prophets and succeed (2 Chronicles 20:20).

PATRICIA KING

INTRODUCTION

*I*n 2017, I had a dream where I heard the voice of God make a loud declaration. He spoke: *"Lana, it's not the end of a season, it's the end of an era,"* and I woke up. The sense surrounded me so strongly that as the body of Christ we were about to enter into a time unlike any other time we had been in before. As I sat with the Lord and I was seeking His heart, I sensed not only one of the greatest shifts upon the body of Christ that we had ever seen or experienced, but an invitation into knowing Him and His heart in a way that we have never experienced before. When you enter into a new era, it is *completely* new. In a moment I understood why the Lord had been repeating Isaiah 43:19 to me over and over again for so long:

Behold, I am doing a new thing; now it springs forth, do you not perceive it? I will make a way in the wilderness and rivers in the desert (ESV).

What He was speaking about and leading us into as the Church was completely new. It suddenly made sense why the Lord had been repeating to me over and over again, *"Everything is about to change."* That's what happens in a new era. Everything changes. It is a total upgrade, new rules, unique supernatural strategies, and we are completely and totally dependent upon His voice to lead us, direct us, and guide us. It is a time when we are invited into a realm of receiving and walking in the wisdom of God in deeper ways. He continued to whisper to me: *"Lana, this is uncharted territory! My people have not been this way before."*

So here we are, a few years later—we have entered into a new era. We have entered into a time unlike any other. We have entered the time when everything changes. We have entered the time when the hand of the Lord is going to move, shift, and build in unprecedented ways. In all that He is going to do, there is an invitation upon us, and that invitation is to go deeper in friendship with God and to know and discover His ways. The Lord showed me that this book is a *feast table of preparation.*

It is a feast set before you by the Lord of what I believe are prophetic keys, strategies, and revelations to help you navigate this new era. This book is a compilation of keys and revelations the Lord has revealed to me to partner with Him in what I believe is going to be the greatest move of the Spirit of God upon the earth that we have ever seen. Preparation is key for this new era. Never in my entire life have I felt the urgency of the hour to be prepared for what the Lord is going to do, like I do now. The Lord is calling the Church to be ready.

It's not complicated. It's not hard. It's not about dotting all your *I*s and crossing all your *T*s. It's about knowing Him, being a friend of God, and being positioned in humility.

I am excited about this journey we are about to embark on together. There will be moments of laughter and joy because of the excitement and expectation of what God is going to do in this new era that you and I get to be a part of. There will be tears, I am sure, as God heals and prepares, and tears of awe and wonder as we see Him and we hear His voice and the revelation of His goodness and majesty is unraveled more and more. There will be moments of challenge, conviction, and pruning. There will be times of impartation, downloads, and encounters with Him that will leave you marked forever.

My heart for you in this book is simply this—that you would see Jesus. That you would encounter His heart. That you would fall more in love with Him than you ever have. That you would hear His voice. That His Spirit would lead you in preparation and navigation of this new era and you would be awakened to your authority and identity in Him in ways you never imagined. That your hunger to know Him and His Word would increase so dramatically that it would lead you deeper into the place of radical abandonment and surrender to Him. That you would know His ways and follow Him in wholehearted obedience. That you would walk in your destiny, follow Him in the uncharted territories, and receive the greatest deliverance of your life from the things that have worked so hard to keep you from all He has for you. That you would take your seat in Christ through revelation of His Word (see Eph. 2:6) and encounter His heart in unprecedented ways. That at the end of the day your greatest testimony would be: "I am a friend of God."

> *There's a private place reserved for the lovers of God, where they sit near him and receive the revelation-secrets of his promises* (Psalm 25:14 TPT).

> *The friendship of the Lord is for those who fear him, and he makes known to them his covenant* (Psalm 25:14 ESV).

Friend, are you ready? Are you ready to step into a place of encounter with Him where everything changes? Let's go together on this journey. I believe in these pages will be one of the greatest adventures of your life with Christ, not because of "Lana Vawser's eloquent words," but because of Jesus and what the Spirit of God is going to do in your life as you read. Position yourself in expectation, faith, and hope! He's about to move!

Chapter One

A GLORIOUS INVITATION

D o you know that there is an invitation from the Lord into your best days? That in this new era there is an invitation from God to step into greater realms and manifestations of your destiny and the plans God has for you in ways you never thought, imagined, or dreamed of? This is an era of acceleration, and there are opportunities, doors, and territories that are completely new awaiting His people. This is an exciting time to be alive. These are the days when the spirit of God is heralding Isaiah 43:19 (ESV), *"Behold, I am doing a new thing...do you not perceive it?"* There is such a call to *perceive* right now. I feel the Spirit of God strongly in this hour calling

His people into the place of having eyes to see and ears to hear and to know the times and the seasons (see Matt. 11:15; 1 Chron. 12:32). The Lord is calling us as His Church to arise in maturity from the place of intimacy with Him to know and understand the hour that we are living in. One of the most important prayers we can pray in this hour is, "Lord, give me wisdom and understanding! Lord, give me discernment." Recently, I had a dream, and the Lord spoke to me: *"Lana, My Spirit of wisdom and revelation is increasing in the earth like never before"* (see Eph. 1:17).

There is an invitation in this new era to walk in the wisdom of God and the revelation of His Word and who He is in depths we have not walked in before. There is an urgency in the invitation because of the magnitude of what God has planned for your life—to do in your life and through your life. This is the hour when the Church will arise in ways we have never seen. This is the hour when you will step into the revelation of your identity like never before as the Spirit of God awakens you to your authority in such deep ways that you will stand before mountains and say *"Move* in the name of Jesus," and they will move because of the power in the name of Jesus and the revelation of who you are in Christ. The key is your position—how you position yourself and where you position yourself.

Many have been in such a battle—some for a few years, others for many years—and it has increased in intensity. If that's you, can I encourage you? You are not alone. The battle has been fierce, the battle has been raging, the battle has been ongoing. Why? Because I believe that the enemy wants to *weary you.* He wants to bring you to a point of such discouragement that you say, "This is too hard," "I can't stand anymore," "It's easier just to lie down." The temptation is huge. Many have been in a place like Elijah, where they have seen God move in power and do great and marvelous things, and all of a sudden they found themselves almost overnight in a season when intimidation has been screaming loudly.

Intimidation

There is an intense demonic assignment of intimidation against the saints in this new era. The enemy continues to attempt to intimidate and bring fear so you will withdraw, so the body of Christ will withdraw. But in the place of battle with this demonic spirit of intimidation, there is a roar being released through you that comes not from what you can conjure or muster up but from the Spirit of God inside of you that roars in faith and says, "I am not stopping, I will not be silent, I will not withdraw until I *see* that which God has promised me *manifest*." Not because I am "hoping" in the natural that it will manifest, but because *God said* it will manifest.

The interesting thing about the intimidation the Lord showed me were His words: *"It is an illusion of intimidation."* The Lord showed me that not only was this intimidation coming with the intention to hinder you moving forward and stepping into the greater revelation of your identity, but it was looking for your worship and to hinder your vision.

Recently, I had a dream. In the dream I watched as a significant number of people were kidnapped by a group of bad guys. As these people were kidnapped, there was such fear that they were going to die. There was such fear and intimidation that if they tried to escape they would be killed. Throughout the whole dream the only thing I could feel was this screaming intimidation. At the end of the dream as God's people were really starting to panic and fear, a man walked up to them. The man was full of peace, with such comfort in his voice, and he spoke: "Relax! It's okay! It's all a game. They are just actors. It's okay." Then I woke up.

When I sat with the Lord and sought His heart on the dream, the Lord spoke to me that many are feeling kidnapped, trapped by fear, intimidation, and other things, and the enemy is just playing games; he's playing tricks to cage them in intimidation. In the dream all vision was stolen from God's people except for the vision of panic, anxiety, and "How do I escape?" What the Lord was saying through that dream was, *"Come up higher. This is all an illusion. The enemy is just playing tricks; you are not really being kidnapped. They are actors; it's an illusion."*

Era of Precision and Vision

This is an era of *precision* in many ways. This is the era when those who are leaning in and have eyes to see and ears to hear will walk in precise vision, precise hearing, precise clarity, precise wisdom, and precise strategy in prayer. The enemy is attempting to *hinder* the era of precision by causing these illusions of intimidation to cause God's people to be *preoccupied!*

This is a time unlike any other to *fight* against distraction! I am going to go more into distraction in another chapter, but I want to encourage you to stand against it! It's easy to see that 2020 is a year of *vision!* This is a year when God is releasing vision, not only for the year of 2020 but for the decade. God is releasing *vision* for longevity. He is releasing *vision* for building with Him long term. He is releasing vision that will affect nations. The Lord spoke to me that this is the year and the era when *history changes!* This is the year and the era when God's people *see* Him like they have never seen Him before, high and lifted up in His Majesty and holiness (see Isa. 6), and *everything changes!*

This is an era of vision and commission, when God reveals significant divine insight and revelation. He shows you what is really going on because many of you have been caught in the web of the enemy's lies, false truths, and deception. God is bringing you into the light of His truth and His Word and showing you the reality of what is going on in the spirit, clearing the haze, clearing your vision so you can see clearly as He sees and then partner with Him in decree and faith to see it manifest upon the earth. The battle is fierce because this is the year and era when *everything changes* as you partner with Him. No wonder the battle and the screaming intimidation.

The Lord was highlighting to me that an illusion is something that you *see*. It's about vision! It is a mirage. It is something that *looks* real but it's not. It is something that screams and screams but it is empty of substance. It doesn't have weight. How could God say it's an illusion? I heard First John 4:4 so loudly in my spirit:

> *Little children, you are from God and have overcome them, for he who is in you is greater than he who is in the world* (ESV).

Friends, I want you to hear this clearly. This is a revelation that God is birthing and growing in you in this new era. This is a revelation that He wants you to capture and wants you to see, for this whole battle is about *you taking your place* in knowing Him and making Him known. It's about *you* walking in your authority and the name of Jesus being glorified in the whole earth. The intimidation is an illusion, because greater is *He* who is in you than he who is in the world. There is an awakening taking place to your authority, and the battle has been so fierce because God is decreeing that as you partner with Him, yield to Him, and allow His Spirit to do its work within you, you are being branded as *unstoppable!*

Divine Reset

Can you see yourself as unstoppable? Maybe the battle has caused you to feel like you are anything *but* unstoppable, but that's where this glorious prophetic word comes in. *This is your time of divine reset.* For many years, the Lord has been speaking to me about the divine reset. I believe that He has been preparing us for reset and He has been continually resetting areas of our hearts and lives that need that divine reset. I heard the Lord say:

"Lana, in this new era many of My people are now left facing the greatest giants of their lives—the ones they have fought almost all their lives. As I have been resetting in many ways over the years, for many the biggest ones have been left till last. Why? Because I am about to display My power in partnering with My people to bring these giants down. That is going to display My faithfulness and My power like never before. That will take them to a new level of faith and awakening that will usher them into walking in the greatest level of signs, wonders, and miracles they have ever seen."

In 2020 and beyond there is such a significant alignment that is taking place by the hand of God that He is bringing forth a divine reset. It is not a reset that you can accomplish by your own hand or effort; it is a divine reset that is only accomplished by the hand of God. This is the *hour of His power* being revealed and demonstrated in your life, through your life, and in the earth like we have never seen before.

You are going to arise in this new era as you live close to Him with a strength, an empowerment of His Spirit, a boldness, and a *roar* inside of you that is louder than ever, that declares, *"I am not moving."* It will be a demonstration of Zechariah 4:6:

> *Then he said to me, "This is the word of the Lord to Zerubbabel: Not by might, nor by power, but by my Spirit, says the Lord of hosts"* (ESV).

I still remember the day I was sitting with Jesus, enjoying my coffee, and just chatting with Him when He spoke to me, *"Lana, I am going to re-introduce the Church to My power in this new era."* What a glorious thing to hear! You will hear me say this a few times in this book because it's so important. God's power is going to be so evident in your life, in the Church, and the earth in this new era that it will not only restore hope in your heart, restore faith, breathe life into you again, and demonstrate His faithfulness, it is going to bring the *greatest and most accelerated alignment of your life thus far.* Deuteronomy 1:11 says this:

> *May the Lord, the God of your fathers, add to you a thousand times as many as you are and bless you, just as He has promised you!* (AMP)

There is a significant alignment that God is going to bring into your life in this new era. Not only will He align what He has promised, He is going to increase you in a way you have never been before. It's not a passive place of sitting back and saying, "Yes Lord, do it all Lord." It's a place of partnering in faith with what He has said and yielding to Him. So it will all be by His power, absolutely. But it does require us to partner in faith and ask the Lord how to position ourselves before Him in this divine reset that He wants to bring into our lives. He is going to demonstrate His faithfulness and His power and bring divine reset and alignment. All the crooked places are going to be made straight. All the things that may be out of alignment and areas where the enemy has continued to maintain legal ground and occupy, the Spirit of God is going to work deeply in hearts and lives to reveal these things and show us how to partner with Him to see this divine reset of His hand manifest in our life.

It's not the Lord sitting in heaven saying, *"Convince Me to do it"* or *"When you get it right, I'll move."* There is a greater work God is doing. He is teaching His people, in deeper ways than ever before, what it looks like to partner with what He is doing and speaking and walk in it, because this is the era of bold faith and supernatural signs, wonders, and miracles that will follow those who *believe*.

Now I want to touch on this for a moment:

> *And these signs will accompany those who believe; in my name they will cast out demons; they will speak in new tongues; they will pick up serpents with their hands; and if they drink any deadly poison, it will not hurt them; they will lay their hands on the sick, and they will recover* (Mark 16:17-18 ESV).

"These signs will accompany those who *believe*." In the battle and in the assault many have faced, the Lord has been working deeply within His people to bring them to a place of greater faith. It's a faith that lives not by natural reality, but it is the faith that lives from the heavenly reality. It's the faith that lives from the place of Matthew 4:4: *"Man shall not live by bread alone, but by every word that proceeds from the mouth of God."* It is a faith that lives from the glorious place of Ephesians 2:6: *"And God raised us up with Christ and seated us with him in the heavenly realms in Christ Jesus"* (NIV). In all that many have walked through in this new era—trials, assaults of the enemy, hardships—in all of it, God is working deeply to bring His people to a deeper place of living by the reality of what He speaks. Living *from* our seat in heavenly places, living *from* victory, and governing from our place of authority in Christ.

There has been a resounding call in the midst of the battles and the struggles. The voice of the Lord has been heard: *"Come up higher! Live higher!"* The pressure of the past seasons and past years has been raising up the Davids who stand before the Goliaths and do not shrink back. They stand up tall and say, *"For who is this uncircumcised Philistine, that he should defy the armies of the living God?"* (1 Sam. 17:26 ESV). It is the ferocious focus of faith, which we will cover more in-depth in another chapter, but this is part of the reset that God is bringing. He is raising up a people who believe, who take Him at His Word, and who stand in front of the giants and declare, "Who do you think you are? Who do you think you are to stand against *my* God? The Lord of heaven and earth? The King of kings and Lord of lords!" That's my paraphrase. It's the awakening of authority within *believers!* Those who *believe!*

Endurance

In the areas where weariness, the battle with intimidation, the sickness, the marriage issues, the financial hardship, the delay, the demonic oppression, the demonic assault, the lack of breakthrough, all of it has wearied you, I want to encourage you. God has been bringing you to a place of deeper trust. He has been working in your heart to bring you up higher. Often in times of deep hardship, we can either give up or dig our heels into the ground, and if you are anything like me you've had moments of both. You give up for a day, then the wind of the Spirt breathes on you again and you're up again. In this battle with intimidation and the hardship of the seasons, God is taking you further away from giving up to the deep conviction inside of you that is getting louder and louder: "I am not taking this anymore! This is not my inheritance! This isn't who I am in Christ and this isn't my portion."

That fire inside of you is going to continue to increase as you stay close to Jesus and deep in His Word. It is going to get stronger and stronger in this new era as you live close to His heart. It's a personal revival. He is branding you as unstoppable, and He is giving you a gift that will last the ages. Yes, I can hear you asking the question already: "Lana, what gift is that?"

Well, I am so glad you asked. Let me tell you what happened in September last year. I was sitting in my prayer room with the Lord, again enjoying my coffee with Him, and He whispered to me: *"Lana, I have a gift for you."*

Oh gosh, was I excited! "Breakthrough! I bet it's breakthrough! What is it, Lord?"

What He spoke next surprised me: *"Lana, it is the gift of endurance."*

Not what I expected to hear.

According to *Merriam-Webster's Dictionary*, *endurance* is "the ability to withstand hardship or adversity, especially the ability to sustain a prolonged stressful effort or activity; the act or an instance of enduring or suffering."

Now as you can imagine, I was left *speechless*. I had certainly endured unpleasant and difficult processes. I certainly at times wanted to give way and certainly felt wear and tear, but in a moment, through an encounter with Him, He opened my eyes. I may have been feeling that way in some areas, I may have been through horrendous battles, but

I keep getting back up again. Somehow, there is something in me that's getting deeper and deeper, stronger and stronger that says, "I ain't moving and I ain't going nowhere. I am standing right here, staring the giant in the face until I see the Word of the Lord manifest in my life because *He is faithful.*"

I then heard the Lord say:

> **"I am teaching My people to live by My Spirit and not by their soul. To live by their soul will cause them to fall; to live by My Spirit will cause them to *endure*."**

In a moment, I was undone. I wept before the Lord, because in the midst of the battles, the hardship of the last few years, the deep pain, grief, and torment I was being awakened to a gift from the hand of the Lord Himself that would last the ages and would not be taken from me. It was the gift of *endurance*. Was it fun? No way! Was it absolutely necessary? Yes! After that encounter, God continued to show me over and over again that His people need to be people of *endurance* and *maturity*. Through all they have been enduring, not only is this the season when God is resetting everything, not only is this the season when God's people will occupy the land of promise and manifestation and step into greater increase than they imagine (see Deut. 1:11), but the Lord was also preparing them with the *endurance* they need to walk in this new era and steward it well as they live close to Him and yield to His ways. What a glorious good, good Father.

> *And so, from the day we heard, we have not ceased to pray for you, asking that you may be filled with the knowledge of his will in all spiritual wisdom and understanding, so*

as to walk in a manner worthy of the Lord, fully pleasing to him: bearing fruit in every good work and increasing in the knowledge of God; being strengthened with all power, according to his glorious might, for all endurance and patience with joy; giving thanks to the Father, who has qualified you to share in the inheritance of the saints in light (Colossians 1:9-12 ESV).

My fellow believers, when it seems as though you are facing nothing but difficulties, see it as an invaluable opportunity to experience the greatest joy that you can! For you know that when your faith is tested it stirs up power within you to endure all things. And then as your endurance grows even stronger, it will release perfection into every part of your being until there is nothing missing and nothing lacking.

Acceleration

God wants you missing and lacking nothing. God wants you strong in Him and fortified in Him, partnering with Him in this mighty wave of the Spirit of God that is going to crash into the earth, ushering in the greatest move of the Spirit of God that we have ever seen. One of the greatest gifts He is giving you in this new era is the gift of endurance. So keep yielding to Him. Keep surrendering and staying close to His heart in faith, allowing Him to do what He needs to do, because He has been preparing you and is preparing you to step into more than you have imagined and dreamed. This is your time of divine reset. This is the time when you are going to see the greatest alignments of your life take place by the power of the Spirit—you and the Lord, hand in hand in partnership—that will leave you in *awe* and *wonder*. You won't even recognize your life in many ways in the fulfillment and acceleration that is going to fall upon your life. This is the era when what would take ten years to do in the natural, God will do in one year. Be expectant for the hand of God to move, because the greatest acceleration you have ever known is upon you right now.

The Lord spoke to me that in this new era the Church is going to come into a deeper place of the revelation of Isaiah 55:11:

> *So shall My word be that goes forth from My mouth; it shall not return to me void, but it shall accomplish what I please, and it shall prosper in the thing for which I sent it.*

This demonic assignment against the people of God through this intimidation and weariness has been to attempt to convince God's people that God isn't faithful. Where the enemy has pushed against God's people, whispering lies about the faithfulness of God, and the weariness has increased, so has the battle to stand in the truth of God's faithfulness. The Lord showed me incredible battles in people's hearts over holding to the revelation of His faithfulness and weariness and faith lost in the faithfulness of God. I want to encourage you as I shared above what the Lord spoke: *"My faithfulness and power will be displayed like never before."* The demonstration of God's faithfulness in your life in this new era is going to *astound* you. The revelation of how faithful He is and the manifestation of that faithfulness is going to heal your heart and bring strength and life to you again. If there is an area of your heart where you have deemed God not faithful, then I encourage you to repent of believing that lie and align yourself with the truth of Scripture again:

> *The steadfast love of the Lord never ceases; his mercies never come to an end; they are new every morning; great is your faithfulness* (Lamentations 3:22-23 ESV).

> *Your love is so extravagant, it reaches higher than the heavens! Your faithfulness is so astonishing, it stretches to the skies!* (Psalm 108:4 TPT)

This is the season when you are going to see mighty demonstrations of Isaiah 55:11. God is going to demonstrate in power that when He speaks, His Word does *not* return void. There is a major shift taking place in the spirit; the Lord is leading you into a deeper place of the revelation of His faithfulness. I heard the Lord say, *"This is the era when My faithfulness will be loud and resound."*

This is the era when God is turning the page. It's a new beginning. It's time for you to believe again. It's time for you to hope again. This is the era when the Spirit of God is bringing such a deep, divine reset in your heart and in your life that you will move into a deep realm of faith that lives, breathes, and walks in Matthew 19:26: *"But Jesus looked at them and said, 'With man this is impossible, but with God all things are possible'"* (ESV).

I want to declare over you today that this is the era when the breath of God is breathing over you and bringing you back to life and into new life (see John 10:10). This is the time when the power of God bringing forth a divine reset in your life is going to cause you to dream again. Not only will the huge, astounding demonstrations of His faithfulness heal your heart and breathe life into you again, but they will cause you to dream again. To dream with God again. To believe again. To not be shackled by disappointment, failure, or regret, but to be full of new vision. Heavenly vision. Heavenly focus. Heavenly excitement to see what He sees for this new era and what He is going to do. As you stay close to His heart and embrace the move of His Spirit, He is raising up the warrior within you.

Unprecedented, Accelerated Answers to Prayer

The Lord showed me that we have entered the era of *accelerated answers to prayer.*

As I sat with the Lord seeking His heart for this chapter, the Lord spoke to me to include a prophetic word that He gave me for this new era as a word for you. This word is not for you to print out and just "leave on the shelf," but it's an invitation for you to engage your faith with Him in expectation because this is the era when you shall see *astonishing* answers to prayer. I encourage you, as you ponder this word, to really let it minister to you. Marinate in it, feast on it, because in this era the answers to prayer the body of Christ shall see will leave us in awe and wonder of who He is. Psalm 65 is burning on my heart:

> *You answer our prayers with amazing wonders and with awe-inspiring displays of power. You are the righteous God who helps us like a father. Everyone everywhere looks to you, for you are the confidence of all the earth, even to the farthest islands of the sea. What jaw-dropping, astounding power is yours! You are the mountain maker who sets them all in place* (Psalm 65:5-6 TPT).

> *You faithfully answer our prayers with awesome deeds, O God our savior. You are the hope of everyone on earth, even those who sail on distant seas. You formed the mountains by your power and armed yourself with mighty strength* (Psalm 65:5-6 NLT).

As I have sat with the Lord in this psalm, God has been speaking to me about how we as the body of Christ have entered into a new era when we shall see *astounding* answers to prayer on a grander scale.

Merriam-Webster's Dictionary gives the following synonyms for *astounding*: amazing, astonishing, blindsiding, dumbfounding, eye-opening, flabbergasting, jarring, jaw-dropping, jolting, shocking, startling, stunning, stupefying, surprising. In this new era, God is going to answer prayers in *astounding* ways. God's power and strength in answer to prayer is going to be demonstrated in *jaw-dropping* ways.

I heard the Lord saying over and over, *"I am turning the table on unanswered prayer."* When I asked the Lord what He meant, I was instantly taken to Daniel 10:13:

> *The prince of the kingdom of Persia withstood me twenty-one days, but Michael, one of the chief princes, came to help me, for I was left there with the kings of Persia* (ESV).

The Lord began to show me many in the body of Christ who have had significant opposition to their prayers and petitions being answered. The enemy has been fighting hard, coming against the promises of God to bring delay. For a long time, I know many, including me, have been heralding a message that "God is breaking delay." The power of delay is breaking in significant ways in the body of Christ, and we have entered a new era when we shall see *astounding answers* to prayer. God is going to show His power and His strength like we have never seen before.

The battle has been so intense over these answers to prayer manifesting in your life because these are the most life-changing answers to prayer you will have ever received.

Birthing Time

The enemy is attempting to hinder prayer times. Push through and intentionally intercede through the distraction and the fog. It's *birthing time!*

The Lord showed me a *huge,* black, hazy cloud, and it was hovering over different places in the body of Christ. When I asked the Lord what it was, He said to me that it was an assignment from the enemy to bring heaviness, distraction, fog, and anything he can to hinder the prayers of the saints to arise. The Lord spoke: *"Now is the time to ferociously and violently intercede, for a great outpouring of answered prayer is about to be released."*

The enemy is coming against prayer times, prayer ministries, and prayer groups to attempt to bring a *hindrance* because the time of the birthing of *major* answers to prayer is upon us. This is the *last push* for many individuals, families, churches, workplaces, cities, and nations to see major fulfillment of His promises in long-awaited places.

The Lord spoke again: *"The answers hang in the balance."* There is a *major* battle over these answers being released upon the earth, but the Lord is giving the *keys to victory.*

The enemy is trying everything to stop these answered prayers being released, but God is going to show Himself strong. He is inviting us to join with Him. He's looking for those who will continue to intercede and take Him at His Word. He's looking for those who will *remind Him* of His Word.

The body of Christ is about to move into the greatest time of being positioned to release the thundering sound upon the earth, *"Jesus is the answer,"* and His wisdom and strategies are the answer. Do not be tempted to "lay down your sword." Hold it tight and *fight!* Don't lie down, *fight!* Be like Elijah in First Kings 18 with your head between your knees in intercession for the *rain.* For the *sound* of rain is being heard and the enemy is raging mad. The heavens are *thundering* with the sound of a glorious outpouring of His rain upon the earth, transforming individual lives, families, cities, and nations.

This is it, friends! This is the *kairos* time (the time of fulfillment, the destined time) that we have been anticipating. It's going to be like nothing we have ever seen or experienced before.

His glory and majesty that will be revealed through these answers to prayer will be blinding and nothing will stay the same. Everything will change as He manifests Himself as the Lion of Judah, the King of kings, the Lord of lords, the God of Ephesians 3:20.

Push! Push! Push! Worship is *key* to break the haze trying to keep you from the place of intercession.

Stay in the place of intercession and faith; let *nothing* distract you, for we have entered the new era of *astounding* answers to prayer like we have *never* seen before.

Friend, this is the era when your greatest days are ahead. This is the era when you leave the past behind. The hand of God is closing the chapter on "what was"—the things that have held you, captured you, contained you, intimidated you—and He is bringing you into the new and what He is doing. This is your new beginning. The Lord showed me a mighty wave of deliverance that will crash into the body of Christ in this new era, ushering the people of God into freedom that has not been known before. Your deliverance is upon you. We will talk more about this later in the book, but I want to encourage you—the story you are stepping into, written by the Lord, will look nothing like the past. It is *so much better* as you partner with Him! It's time! The *kairos* time has arrived. You are moving into the place of occupying. This is the era when the demonstration of His faithfulness in and through your life will be louder than ever. This is the restoration, recompense, retribution, and justice of God demonstrated.

This is when you see the *astounding* demonstration of His faithfulness in unprecedented ways. This is the point where everything changes!

Chapter Two

A CALL TO
THE UPPER ROOM

*T*here is a weighty call from the Lord into the upper room in this new era. We cannot, as God's people, move into the season of the greatest acceleration of His Spirit upon the earth and in the Church if we are not living from the upper room. Recently I heard the Lord say, *"Come into the upper room; My fire is falling for the new frontiers and uncharted territories."*

There is a fresh impartation of faith and boldness that is coming to the *upper room* from the Lord to go and do that which He has called us to do. It is a fresh impartation to move into places we have never moved in before; it is a fresh boldness to speak and preach the Gospel with boldness. It is the place where fear loses it legs and you are totally overcome and immersed in the boldness that comes from knowing Him. And that's the key—knowing Him and the power of His Spirit.

Whenever I think of the "upper room" I think of the place of encounter and empowerment. As I have sat with the Lord pondering the invitation into the upper room in this new era, those two words are key—*encounter* and *empowerment*. The verse resounding loudly in my spirit is Acts 4:31:

> *And when they had prayed, the place in which they were gathered together was shaken, and they were all filled with the Holy Spirit and continued to speak the word of God with boldness* (ESV).

This is the hour of His power. This is the era of being reintroduced to the power of God. This is the era of the days of *acts* and *beyond*.

His words surrounded me: *"It's the era of mighty acts, the era of My outstretched arm!"*

> *With his mighty power he brought them out! His tender love for us continues on forever!* (Psalm 136:12 TPT)

> *And the Lord brought us out of Egypt with a mighty hand and an outstretched arm, with great deeds of terror, with signs and wonders* (Deuteronomy 26:8 ESV).

The fresh encounters with Jesus, the fresh impartation of faith and empowerment of the Holy Spirit are happening in the upper room as His people wait on Him. The Lord showed me many will be dazzled by the season of opportunity and pursue "fame for their name" and put their hands to "much" for the Lord, but the breath of God will not be upon their works.

The Lord showed me that those who are lingering in the upper room in this new era will carry the *breath of God* that will bring signs, wonders, and miracles never seen before.

The shaking of Acts 4:31 is beginning to rumble. It is the fresh commissioning for the new frontier. It is the place of the greatest empowerment of the Spirit that has never been walked in before. It is the place of receiving a supernatural boldness that has never before been carried to go, build, say, and obey all the Lord is commanding. The invitation into the upper room is resounding louder than ever for this new apostolic age. Don't get so caught up in this era of opportunity and acceleration that you miss Him, because He is coming, ready or not.

This deep place of encounter awaiting us in this new era is where there is a fresh commissioning taking place for the new assignments that the Lord has for us, and it is taking place in the upper room. This invitation is to leave behind the noise and distractions and to come into the place of prayer, communion, and lingering with Him. The fire of God is falling, and the Spirit of God is going to continue to fall in such power. It will cause everything that can be shaken to be shaken.

Mighty deliverances are going to take place in the upper room. There will be sudden deliverances, sudden healing, sudden alignment, sudden shift of vision, and supernatural alignment that is going to take place.

> "In order for My people to move into the new frontiers, they must be in the upper room to receive the *fresh fire*."

When the Lord spoke "fresh fire," I felt everything shake in the spirit. There is *fresh fire* the Lord is releasing upon His people who come into the upper room of prayer and wait upon Him, and it is going to be fresh fire for the *pioneering* that is before them. A fresh impartation of boldness, passion, and hunger to know Him deeper than ever is found in the upper room.

Answer the Call to the Upper Room

The urgency to answer the call to the upper room gripped me. I felt the longing heart of the Lord so strongly. Where you are going, where we are going, we have never been before. Where the Lord is sending His people in this new apostolic age, the age of the Kingdom, we haven't been before. I heard the Lord say, "*You cannot go as you are.*" The journey ahead requires a fresh baptism of His fire. It requires a fresh impartation of faith. It requires the place of fresh encounters with the Lord. It's the place of stepping completely and totally into the *new* to move into where He is going. It's a complete shedding and shaking off of the old.

The encounters with Jesus in the upper room are going to be revolutionary. It is the place where the Lord is going to download His wisdom and teach His people His ways and give them understanding of His ways on a scale we haven't encountered before (see Ps. 119:23-24).

In this encounter I saw the new frontier ahead, the uncharted territories, and there was a keyhole to be passed through to enter into these new frontiers. I asked the Lord what the key is, and I heard the Lord say: "*It's the upper room.*"

Everything that is needed will flow *in* and *from* the upper room. In this season of unprecedented acceleration, pioneering and extending and building the Kingdom of God with Him, it requires *much* prayer and fasting and *waiting/lingering* with the Lord.

It is the season to *run,* but it is the season to run with the Lord *from* the upper room. There is a weighty empowerment coming. The fire of God is going to come in such a powerful way, bringing a refining, a strengthening, a purging and a purifying to run in holiness and truth. The fire of His presence is going to fall in this new era in such a way that the *burning ones* are going to be sent forth into the earth carrying His wisdom and revelation for the new era, to release the fire of His presence and His power, ushering in the greatest demonstration of His power and revelation of His Glory that the Church has ever seen.

It is the fiery, burning heart of the love of God that is going to brand His people who meet Him in the upper room afresh. God wants *everyone* in His Church to be part of this glorious move of His Spirit. The Lord is inviting all to come and to meet with Him to feast with Him, to commune with Him, but it is those who will answer His invitation who will run with Him into the new thing that He is doing (see Isa. 43:19). For this era is an era of the line in the sand. It's the place where you are either all in or you aren't. This is the era when adoration and devotion will be revealed. This is the era when the mighty acceleration will reveal the greatest adoration and devotion of the heart. This is the era when there will be a great exposing of what is in the heart.

Does God reveal what is in the heart to condemn? Absolutely not! It's out of His love that He reveals what is in the heart, and this call into the upper room like never before is going to reveal what is in the heart. It is going to expose other loves, idols, and areas of devotion before the Lord. To carry what the Lord is releasing in this new era is going to cost something. It is going to look different, and it is going to cause a pruning of what was and an entering into what *is.* When the

Lord releases a weighty invitation and there's a battle of the heart, it's the decisions that are made in those places that matter.

Is the invitation into the upper room of prayer and waiting on Him available to all? Yes! But what do we do with that invitation? Where do we allow our devotion and adoration to fall in this new era? It's time to let go of any other loves and idols and come into the upper room and wait on Him. It's time for the returning to the first love (see Rev. 2:4).

"Look into My Eyes and See the Age Ahead"

As this encounter continued, I saw Jesus standing before me, and His eyes were like flames of fire. He spoke: *"Look into My eyes and see the age ahead."*

> *His eyes are like a flame of fire, and on his head are many diadems, and he has a name written that no one knows but himself* (Revelation 19:12 ESV).

The words began to come out of my mouth: "There are encounters with His eyes in the upper room. There are encounters with His eyes in the upper room." I began to weep as I saw Him. The whole room was full of the bright shining light of His Glory and the revelation of Jesus Christ opening up and exploding in the upper room. The Lord spoke again:

> "The revelation of My glory and the revealing of who I am in this new apostolic age is going to mark My people and transform My people. It is the great undoing. It's the reformation in the revealing of who I am. In the upper room you will be *marked by love*! You will be marked by the fire of My love again!"

I see upper rooms all over the earth filled with people on their faces crying out, weeping, undone, groaning at the revelation of Jesus. Undone by the weight of His glory and power. He spoke again:

> "In the revealing of who I am is the invitation to see Me and look into My eyes and see the age ahead and to walk in My wisdom and My ways. Out of the encounters with Me in the upper room will come the greatest divine innovations of the new era! In the encounters with Me in the upper room My people will have **ears** for the **new era**."

It's in looking straight into the face of Jesus, in these encounters with the Lord in the upper room, that the revealing of who He is in greater ways will explode. I see the upper rooms being filled with His glory and light exploding out of the windows. I see supernatural manifestations of His light being seen through windows in the natural and people being drawn to see this light exploding from physical buildings and rooms. I see them being drawn in and coming to know Jesus. It will happen in houses, in churches, in buildings. His glory and light will be physically seen.

It is in the upper room, encountering Jesus and looking in His eyes, that the revelation of this apostolic age will come. The revelation of this Kingdom age will come by looking into the face of Jesus. Looking into His eyes. Feasting on the Word, as He is the Word.

As I looked closer in His eyes, I could see flames of fire and I could see pathways and blueprint strategies. In His eyes I could see wisdom. In His eyes I could see His ways. In His eyes I could see glimpses of what was to come in this Kingdom age. He spoke again:

> "If My people will just stop, linger, seek, and pray in this new era and set aside distraction, they will see what is to come in Me in greater ways. Leave behind your mind of what you think it should be like; just be with Me and you will **see**. Be with Me and you will see and rise up as the *eagle*. The commissioning of the eagles will take place from the upper room."

Those words shook me deeply. The commissioning of the eagles will take place from the upper room. He will send out the eagles from the upper room filled with fire, marked by the revelation of Jesus, with eyes that see with prophetic vision and clarity for this new era we have entered.

I then looked at the eyes of the eagles, and their eyes blazed with heavenly sight. In the upper room, in looking in the eyes of Jesus, the One whose eyes were like flames of fire, they had received such an upgrade of sight in the spirit, they were being sent forth with a heavenly *insight* and *hindsight* for this new era. I heard Him speak again:

> "These eagles will be sent forth to uncover and reveal My truth."

These eagles were being sent forth with eyes of Daniel 2:22:

> *He reveals deep and hidden things; he knows what is in the darkness, and the light dwells with him* (ESV).

These eagles were going forth with such wisdom, discernment, and divine insight and hindsight. They were going forth to uncover that which is darkness and to reveal truth—His truth. To bring forth the establishment of truth, heavenly truth, in this new era. They were going forth with prophetic insight and hindsight to bring alignment and to herald the truth of God's Word. This apostolic company that will arise on the earth has their eyes locked with His eyes. They have eyes that look not to the left or to the right; they have their eyes firmly fixed upon Jesus. They have not given their hearts of love and affection to another.

The Watchman Anointing Will Increase from the Upper Room

From the upper room, the watchman anointing is going to increase more than ever. The heralding of the watchman is going to get louder in this hour in prayer, intercession, and proclamation to bring the body of Christ into a greater position of victory and movement from defense to offense.

> *Son of man, I have made you a watchman for the house of Israel; therefore hear a word from My mouth, and give them warning from Me* (Ezekiel 3:17).

As I continued to seek the Lord, I saw the words before my eyes: "upper room—upper realm." The sense surrounded me strongly of the bursting forth of the miraculous unlike anything we have ever seen before. The bursting forth of the supernatural into the natural like never before. Unusual signs, wonders, and miracles. The Church walking in greater authority, power, and boldness and living above their natural circumstances and walking on the Word of God. Acts 9:39-40 says:

Peter rose and went with them. And when he arrived, they took him to the upper room. All the widows stood beside him weeping and showing tunics and other garments that Dorcas made while she was with them. But Peter put them all outside and knelt down and prayed; and turning to the body he said, "Tabitha, arise." And she opened her eyes, and when she saw Peter she sat up (ESV).

As we encounter Him in the upper room (see Acts 4:31), we will be empowered by Him to move in the power of the Spirit like never before. We will walk in resurrection power, in boldness, in the authority of Christ to see natural means bow to the name of Jesus Christ.

What I find interesting in verses 39-40 is the widows who stood beside Peter weeping. What were they doing? They were showing him tunics and other garments that Dorcas made while she was with them. Instantly, when I read that verse, the Lord says to me, *"They had not eyes to see. They had not the eyes of faith."*

Gosh, did that hit me. Keep reading. It doesn't say, "Peter gave them a hug and told them everything would be okay." It says, *"Peter put them all outside, and knelt down and prayed."* The New International Version says it this way: *"Peter sent them all out of the room; then he got down on his knees and prayed."*

I believe that there is a very strong warning and encouragement from the Lord for this new era in this verse. The Lord is encouraging us as we live *from* the upper room and move *into* these realms of signs, wonders, and miracles that we are on a scale that we have never seen before. We have to "put out" and "do away with" *anything* that is contrary to the Word of God and the will of God. We have to be in the place of faith like never before, and that place of faith comes from lingering in the upper room with Him, waiting on Him, knowing Him, meditating on His Word. We see Him in His glory, the continual unravelling revelation of Jesus; we are changed and taken into a new realm of faith. In this place of living in the revelation of who Jesus is, the shackles to living in deeper realms of faith will fall away.

I also felt the weight of the Lord upon this passage to have "eyes to see." The widows' focus was upon their grief of Dorcas' death. Were the widows believers? We aren't told that specifically. It seems they were, but what we are told is that their focus was upon tunics, clothes, and robes and their grief at Dorcas' passing.

This era is about walking in bold faith. This theme continues and will continue to run through all of this book. Why? Because the Lord's heart is for us to walk in authority and victory like never before and take Him at His Word.

So in these "upper room" encounters in this new era, the fresh fire and impartation of the Lord will come upon you to walk in bold faith, to walk in the miraculous and see His power explode in and through your life in ways you have not thought, imagined, or dreamed (see 1 Cor. 2:9; Eph. 3:20). It comes with the invitation and exhortation from the Lord that your eyes *must* be fixed on Jesus' eyes.

In this encounter, the Lord spoke, "*Look into My eyes and see the age ahead.*" So in these "upper room" encounters with the Lord you are going to see through the eyes of faith (see 2 Cor. 5:17), and you will see the divine strategy, blueprints, answers, innovations, wisdom, and insight of what the Lord is going to do in this new era so you can partner with it.

One of the greatest battles in this new era will be over the eyes— when things happen in the natural that are dark, tragic, and difficult. When you are standing in faith and moving in the Word of the Lord and other people show you things in the natural that are not in line with what God is about to do.

If I could sum up this chapter in a few words, do you know what I would say? I would say, "Run into the upper room. Not just once. Continually. Keep your gaze on Him and His eyes. Be positioned, whatever it takes, to meet with Him. Let your top priority be to know Jesus and be hungry to know Him. Don't move from the place of lingering before Him. Those who linger, He will entrust the secrets of His heart."

Throw Off Distraction

I want to encourage you to get fierce with distractions in this new era because the enemy will continue to do all he can to distract you from the upper room and from living in the place of bold faith. I look at the story of Peter and Dorcas and I think, "The widows were a distraction." Were they intentionally trying to distract? Of course not! Could you imagine Peter trying to pray for Dorcas to be raised from the dead with the widows in the room? How distracting. Do not tolerate distraction in this new era.

I want to encourage you with this as well. The Lord spoke to me about the power of His Spirit that will flow through those who linger in the upper room and move in radical faith in this new era. It will cause others to be awakened in their faith.

> *Peter sent them all out of the room; then he got down on his knees and prayed. Turning toward the dead woman, he said, "Tabitha, get up." She opened her eyes, and seeing Peter she sat up. He took her by the hand and helped her to her feet. Then he called for the believers, **especially the widows,** and presented her to them alive. This became known all over*

Joppa, and many people believed in the Lord (Acts 9:40-42 NIV).

The demonstration of the Lord's power through your life as you walk by faith and not by sight in this new era, as your eyes are fixed to His eyes and you walk by His gaze, will cause a revival and awakening in others around you. The testimonies of the power of God that you will have in this new era, you cannot even imagine or fathom yet. The realm of "nothing is impossible for those who believe" that you will walk in will be unprecedented (see Mark 9:23).

To live *in* the upper room and *from* the upper room is upon us now. Greater than what was seen in the book of Acts. Above and beyond. Glory to glory. This incredible, history-changing, earth-shaking move of the Spirit of God and demonstration of His power and unveiling of Jesus is available and accessible to *all* His children, but it will be *walked in* by those who live in the upper room, those who linger with Him and are truly friends of God.

Chapter Three

KATHRYN KUHLMAN'S LIFE: A KEY FOR THIS NEW ERA

For many years now, the Lord has been speaking to me about the major demonstrations of His healing power that are going to be seen in the new era that we have entered. As the Lord has spoken this to me over the years, He has continually highlighted Kathryn Kuhlman to me. If you are not familiar with Kathryn Kuhlman, she lived from 1907 to 1976, and she was an evangelist known for her healing services.

I came across a quote of Kathryn's taken from *A Glimpse into Glory,* and I want to share it with you. I want you to really take a moment and read this carefully and allow the Holy Spirit to minister to you, because in Kathryn's words there are keys of wisdom and revelation for this new era we have entered:

> There are literally thousands and thousands in the great charismatic movement who have never become acquainted with the person of the Holy Spirit, only with His gifts.[1]

Kathryn Kuhlman referred to the Holy Spirit as her "best friend." She is also quoted:

> "He knows that I will be true to Him as long as my old heart keeps beating, and I know that I will be true to Christ. We have a pact.
>
> "...All He needs is somebody who will die, and when I died, He came in. I was baptized. I was filled with the Spirit. I spoke in an unknown tongue as He took every part of me. In that moment, I surrendered unto Him all there was of me, everything. Everything. Then, for the first time I realized what it meant to have power."
>
> [Kathryn] often spoke of the responsibility of being entrusted by the Holy Spirit with the administration of His gifts, particularly with the kind of ministry she had. She trembled at the thought of grieving Him. She knew that He is a literal person, and that the only way to be used by Him was to follow Him.
>
> Many times in her messages, Miss Kuhlman warned Christians not to try to "use" the Holy Spirit, but only to let Him *lead* them. His power, she said, is under His sole authority, not ours. She insisted that a Christian can be

yielded enough to the Holy Spirit until there is nothing left of one's self.

"You have to be dead," she would say, because there cannot be two different wills or two conflicting personalities involved. There must be only one, and that one is His alone.[2]

Kathryn Kuhlman had a healing ministry during a time when there were many Voice of Healing evangelists, but she operated apart from her contemporaries. She felt that they used too much showmanship and would blame the sick if they were not healed. Kathryn didn't distribute prayer cards or form healing lines. She wanted people to pray and fast, to demonstrate faith with action. She didn't even usually pray for people personally. She just created an atmosphere of worship and faith, and people received their healing.

Kathryn believed the greatest miracles transpired in worship as the Holy Spirit sovereignly moved through the auditorium. The "circus sideshow" and tent theatrics were unnecessary. Bill Johnson writes in his book *Defining Moments*:

> Kathryn realized that simply by honoring the Holy Spirit and by being in God's presence, healing could be released.
>
> "The Holy Spirit, then, was the answer, an answer so profound that no human being can fathom the full extent of its depths and power, and yet so simple that most folk miss it! I understood that night why there was no need for a healing line; no healing virtue in a card or a personality; no necessity for wild exhortations "to have faith." That was the beginning of this healing ministry which God has given me; strange to some because of the fact that hundreds have been healed just sitting quietly in the

audience, without any demonstration whatsoever, and even without admonition. This is because the Presence of the Holy Spirit has been in such abundance that by His Presence alone, sick bodies are healed, even as people wait on the outside of the building for the doors to open."

Even though great healing was released through her ministry, Kathryn, like Carrie Judd Montgomery and many other healing revivalists, denied having a gift of healing. In response to the question of whether she had the gift of healing, she said:

"I would never say that I have ever received any gift. The greatest of the Christian graces is humility. All I know is that I have yielded my body to Him to be filled with the Holy Spirit, and anything that the Holy Spirit has given me, any results there might be in this life of mine, is not Kathryn Kuhlman. It's the Holy Spirit; it's what the Holy Spirit does through a yielded vessel. That is one thing I am so afraid of: I am afraid lest I grieve the Holy Spirit, for when the Holy Spirit is lifted from me I am the most ordinary person that ever lived.

"As I have said before, I am not a faith healer. I have not been given anything special. What I have is something that any Christian could have if he would pay the price of full surrender and yieldedness. I am absolutely dependent on the mercy of the Lord Jesus Christ."[3]

The Lord brought these quotes to my attention because there are keys for this new era in the life of Kathryn Kuhlman. Kathryn Kuhlman was not only known for the amazing miracles that followed her, but she was a plumb line. She was a bold voice of purity calling

God's people into the place of consecration and deep, abiding yielding to Him. I remember hearing a message of hers online, and her call to people was to "die today"—to die to self, to let go of idols, and to come to the place of life, of deep surrender. People came to the front weeping and wailing in repentance as they encountered His love and the weight of His presence that brought them deeper into the place of alignment with the Holy Spirit and Jesus as their first love, the place of life found in Christ.

Over the years, I have been so impacted by Kathryn's humility, yieldedness, purity, and the deepest one I felt the Lord wanted me to focus on here was her *intimacy*. Her focus was not the signs, wonders, and miracles. She lived from the place of friendship with God where the Holy Spirit was her best friend. She lived deeply in the fear of the Lord; she would tremble at the thought of grieving Him.

In this wonderful outpouring in this new era, the healing wave that we will see take place is going to be astounding, but it will be one that will flow from the place of intimacy and friendship with Jesus. The alignment that is taking place and will continue to take place is to rapidly bring the Church deeper into the place of honoring the presence of God without "using" Him.

"I Will Take Center Stage Again"

The Holy Spirit showed me many months ago that "man" was on center stage in many ways. There has been an attribution of glory to titles and to "look at my ministry." The hand of God is coming in such a profound way to bring a significant alignment and recalibration. As the Lord whispered to me, *"I will take center stage again."*

I am not saying that God is not going to heal in prayer lines or healing lines or through the laying on of hands, but I believe that there is going to be a major increase of the power of God in the adoration of who He is. His presence and His worship are going to bring a right focus back to the Church. Jesus is going to take His rightful place again. There has been a "touching of His glory" and a "taking of His glory" in titles and in what Kathryn often described as "showmanship" or "circus sideshow." But the Lord is going to fall so sovereignly and supernaturally in greater increase to *remind* the Church that it is not by any human power that signs, wonders, and miracles come, but through the power of His Spirit and the presence of God.

The wave of His healing is going to mark this era. Those who live in deep intimacy with the Holy Spirit in and from the fear of God will see some of the greatest signs, wonders, and miracles. The wave of healing that is going to crash into the body of Christ will not only be the greatest healing revival and outpouring we have ever witnessed, but it will be carried by those who walk in purity of heart and are friends of God. The move of His Spirit is going to bring forth a mighty purging and purifying, and Jesus is going to take the stage again, where He will get the glory.

Now, this is not to say that the whole body of Christ and all those who move in the gift of healing have fallen. That is not accurate at all. There are many wonderful leaders, ministers, and people of God moving in stunning healing ministries who are walking in purity, integrity, and friendship with the Holy Spirit, but there are obviously areas in the Church where this "taking the glory" has become a very serious issue that the Lord wants to deal with. In those places, He is going to deal with it, calling His people back to the place of repentance. Any focus upon man, any impurity, sin, or manipulation in these movements will be exposed and purified as the Lord brings the alignment and focus back on Jesus and His presence.

He wants to remind the Church that the power of the Holy Spirit is not just available to those who have great influence in the Church. He wants to remind the people of God that *every* person who has the Holy Spirit living inside of them can walk in His power to heal the sick, raise the dead, and cast out demons (see Matt. 10:8).

"You Ain't Seen Nothing Yet"

I have been hearing the Holy Spirit for over two years now whispering to me, "*You ain't seen nothing yet.*" It was such a strong feeling of not having even scratched the surface of what He is going to do and what we are going to see Him do. The healings we have seen Him perform in the earth and in the Church have been amazing, and there are countless millions of testimonies of God's healing power increasing. But can I suggest, compared to what is coming, *we ain't seen nothing yet.*

The major outpouring of healing that is going to take place in this new era will be in astronomical proportions compared to what we have seen, and it will be marked by intimacy with Jesus in ways we have never seen. We are not going to see an exact replica of Kathryn Kuhlman's ministry. There's a new wave coming, but God is highlighting her life because of the fear of the Lord she walked in. Kathryn Kuhlman lived in constant communion and communication with the Holy Spirit and the purity and boldness she carried was inspiring, and that impartation is going to be released into the Church in this new era in ways we have never seen before. The cry of her heart resounded so loudly that Benny Hinn shared this in his book *Good Morning, Holy Spirit*:

> As the service continued and I quietly prayed, everything stopped suddenly. I thought "Please, Lord, don't ever let this meeting end."

I looked up to see Kathryn burying her head in her hands as she began to sob. She sobbed and sobbed so loudly that everything came to a standstill. The music stopped. The ushers froze in their positions.

Everyone had their eyes on her. And for the life of me I had no idea why she was sobbing. I had never seen a minister do that before. What was she crying about? (I was told later that she had never done anything like that before, and members of her staff remember to this day.)

It continued for what seemed like two minutes. Then she thrust back her head. There she was, just a few feet in front of me. Her eyes were aflame. She was *alive*.

In that instant she took on a boldness I had never seen in any person. She pointed her finger straight out with enormous power and emotion—even pain. If the devil himself had been there, she would have flicked him aside with just a tap.

It was a moment of incredible dimension. Still sobbing, she looked out at the audience and said with such agony, "Please." She seemed to stretch out the word, "Plee-ease, *don't grieve the Holy Spirit.*"

She was begging. If you can imagine a mother pleading with a killer not to shoot her baby, it was like that. She begged and pleaded.

"Please," she sobbed, "don't grieve the Holy Spirit."

Even now I can see her eyes. It was as if they were looking straight at me.

And when she said it, you could have dropped a pin and heard it. I was afraid to breathe. I didn't move a muscle. I was holding on to the pew in front of me wondering what would happen next.

Then she said, "Don't you understand? He's all I've got!"

I thought, "What's she talking about?"

Then she continued her impassioned plea saying, "Please! Don't wound Him. He's all I've got. Don't wound the One I love!"

I'll never forget those words. I can still remember the intensity of her breathing when she said them.[4]

Her cry was, "Please don't grieve Him, please don't wound Him!" That purity of intimacy, that purity of communion with the Holy Spirit and reverence for who He is and His presence, that place of deep intimacy is going to be a marker in this great healing outpouring that's coming. The sole, pure focus upon Jesus! Those who treat His heart with care.

Proper Alignment of the Heart and Life

God is using the life of Kathryn Kuhlman again to remind us of the proper alignment of the heart and life. The signs, wonders, and miracles are amazing and will be astounding, but if the *use* of gifting takes the place of deep communion with the Holy Spirit, then there's a problem. There is a danger that can be fallen into in this new era through what God is going to do, and that is to make signs, wonders, and miracles the main thing. Jesus is the main thing—nothing else but Jesus and seeing His name glorified. God is going to take the focus on man out of the body of Christ in many ways in this new era and put it back on Jesus. God's heart is to bring the Church deeper and back to this place.

Was Kathryn Kuhlman perfect? No, none of us are. Kathryn Kuhlman's ministry was marked with miracles, but the legacy she left behind is not just one of amazing miracles but one of a woman who was completely yielded and surrendered to Him, the Holy Spirit, as her best friend. From that place, she saw incredible signs, wonders, and miracles. She didn't leave the stage and come away and out of that anointing. You just have to read about her life and her ministry to see she lived in that place all the time. We are going to see that more and more in this new era as the fire of God purifies and purges, and we will see a greater alignment into this place of purity of relationship with Jesus in the body of Christ.

Kathryn's life, ministry, and purity show what God can do with a laid-down life. It's an invitation for you and me to step into. Not to be "copycats" of Kathryn Kuhlman, but to take the keys and treasures God placed within her life as keys and foundational stones of what is coming and how to steward it.

Notes

1. Kathryn Kuhlman and Jamie Buckingham, *A Glimpse into Glory* (Alachua, FL: Bridge-Logos, 1983), 102.

2. "An Hour with Kathryn Kuhlman," qtd. in Roberts Liardon, *Kathryn Kuhlman: A Spiritual Biography of God's Miracle Worker* (New Kensington, PA: Whitaker House, 2005), Chapter 7.

3. Kathryn Kuhlman, *I Believe in Miracles* (Eaglewood Cliffs, NJ: Prentice-Hall, Inc., 1962), 197-198; and "Healing in the Spirit," *Christianity Today*, July 20, 1973, 5,9; qtd. in Bill Johnson with Jennifer Miskov, *Defining Moments: Kathryn Kuhlman: Hosting the Presence* (New Kensington PA: Whittaker House, 2016), 238-239.

4. Benny Hinn, *Good Morning, Holy Spirit* (Nashville, TN: Thomas Nelson, 1997), 8-9.

Chapter Four

EMBRACING THE CHANGING TONES OF GOD

*T*here is such a weighty invitation and directive from the Lord in this new era to camp around His presence. To camp around where He is moving, where He is breathing, what He is building, and what He is doing. Not in any other season before have I felt the weightiness of this invitation to make room for Him.

> *Put the Levites in charge of the Tabernacle of the Covenant, along with all its furnishings and equipment. They must carry the Tabernacle and all its*

furnishings as you travel, and they must take care of it and camp around it (Numbers 1:50 NLT).

Numbers 1:50 shows how Israel camped around the presence of God. There is a shaking, a realigning, and a recalibrating that is taking place in this new era, bringing the people of God back to the place of camping around His presence. What does it look like to camp around the presence of God? I believe it is a place of positioning. It is a place of surrender; it is a place of humility. It's a place of *making room* and *letting God be God*. That's an interesting concept isn't it? "Let God be God"—like we can somehow stop Him from being God. Psalm 115:3 says:

Our God is in heaven; he does whatever pleases him (NIV).

But we know our God rules from the heavens and he takes delight in all that He does (TPT).

God is God and He does as He pleases, but our positioning and making room for Him in our lives brings us to a place of partnership with Him in all He is doing in the earth so that we don't miss moving with Him.

Examine Our Hearts

I believe in this new era that God is inviting us to examine our hearts and our lives in the light of His presence (see Ps. 139:23-24) and allow Him to reveal what we are camping around and what we are setting up our lives around. That is not navel gazing and being introspective; it's about positioning ourselves before the Lord to invite the Holy Spirit to come and examine our hearts and let *Him* bring to the surface anything that needs to be dealt with.

In this new era we have moved into, we are going to see the greatest move of the Spirit of God in the earth. We need to really sit down with the Holy Spirit and examine the boundary lines we have set up in our lives. What is our true north?

In this new era, there is going to be a major revealing that is going to expose the areas of hearts and lives where things are out of alignment. The Spirit of God is going to bring forth a conviction upon His people that is stronger than we have experienced before. It is going to be the purging before the manifested outpouring.

Are we in the era of the outpouring? Absolutely. Have we entered the time of the Church's greatest days? Yes! Have we entered into the time of seeing the greater glory of God manifesting in the earth like never before? Yes! Yes! Yes! Have we entered an era when we will be reintroduced to the power of God and see miracles beyond our wildest imagination? Indeed we have. But what we need to understand as God's people is that there are going to be wonderful demonstrations of the power of God and a mighty harvest, but there is also a shaking in the Church that has begun and is going to increase significantly to bring the "dross" to the surface in ways we have not seen before.

There is going to be such a deep purging that is going to take place in the Church by the fire of God and the conviction of the Holy Spirit. It is going to prepare the Church to carry what the Lord is releasing. Is the Lord coming, ready or not? Yes, He is.

I have had numerous encounters, visions, and dreams from the Lord where He has showed me that there has been such a celebration and excitement that He is coming, which He is, but the Lord showed me that those who do not have eyes to see and ears to hear are not walking in maturity and are not seeing the full picture. Now, am I saying that I have the full picture? Absolutely not. Am I pointing the finger at anyone, saying, "You're immature"? No way! What I am saying is from the revelation that the Lord has given me there are many in the Church who are only seeing "half the picture." There is a wave of the conviction of the Holy Spirit and the fire of His love that is coming in such a heavy and weighty way that it is going to bring a purging and a greater exposure of sin in the Church. Yes, there is a place of extreme excitement and anticipation about what God is going to do and what He is doing, but there is also a very serious place in this era as well. Like no other time, it is it so important to recognize the "times and seasons" in which we live.

The Call to Consecration

Part of the call to set up camp around the presence of God is to embrace the purging that is going to take place in the body of Christ. It is the call to holiness. It is the call to consecration.

> *Then Joshua said to the people, "Consecrate yourselves, for tomorrow the Lord will do wonders among you"* (Joshua 3:5 ESV).

What we are going to see in this new era is not a light thing; it is not something that can be carried if I have one foot in the world and one in the Kingdom. The move of God that is going to take place on the earth in this new era is going to be the greatest we have seen. It is going to be the revealing of Jesus Christ in His glory and in His majesty that is going to bring in a harvest beyond what we have even imagined. I heard the Holy Spirit say recently:

"Lana, this is the era when the secrets of My heart will be revealed and manifested in the earth like never before. This is the era when Daniel 2:22 will unfold and manifest in greater ways than My people have seen. The power of My hand will be seen to build up and tear down, to draw near and to cast away, to cause to multiply and cause to purify. The movement of My hand to establish My Kingdom will be the greatest that has ever been seen. There have been many great revivalists in history and mighty moves of My hand, and I have done great things. I am going to do in this new era even greater things than have been seen with great revivalists and even in the book of Acts. I am preparing My Church to carry this move. I am coming, ready or not. I am going to move in power and I am going to purify My Church and My Bride in this new era. My tone in changing and I am calling her out of My love to the place of being ready and making herself *ready* for Me and My Spirit moving in unprecedented ways."

He reveals deep and hidden things; he knows what is in the darkness, and the light dwells with him (Daniel 2:22 ESV).

The Lord is going to reveal the deep and hidden things, the glorious deeper revelation of His Word, His wisdom in magnificent ways, His secrets and revelation of His ways. He will also expose and uncover the things hidden in darkness. He will uncover and expose the areas of sin, alignment with the enemy, and compromise in the Church and then in the world in greater ways.

Judgment Begins in the House of God

There is a contamination that has come into the Church that has opened the door to some serious demonic strongholds within the body of Christ. In 2019, the Lord spoke to me in a dream, and He said, *"Judgment begins in the house of God."* That's where I believe we are right now.

> *For it is time for judgment to begin at the household of God; and if it begins with us, what will be the outcome for those who do not obey the gospel of God?* (1 Peter 4:17 ESV)
>
> *For the time is ripe for judgment to begin in God's own household. And if it starts with us, what will be the fate of those who refuse to obey the gospel of God?* (1 Peter 4:17 TPT)

I want you to hear this before I go on.

We stand righteous in Christ (see Rom. 5:1-11). We can approach the throne boldly because of the death and resurrection of Jesus Christ and there is nothing, absolutely nothing that can separate us from His love (see Rom. 8:31-39). It is *because of His love* that He is bringing a purification, a purging, and a shaking. It is *because* of His kindness that He is bringing forth a purifying fire and an exposing, so we can walk in the light and walk in all that He has for us. It is because He wants *all* of His people to be partnered with what He is doing and going to do on the earth that He is bringing forth this mighty shaking. It *has* to take place; we cannot go forward as we are. The Church in many ways has drifted so far away from the first love of Jesus and the Gospel and He is bringing that back. He is bringing forth an alignment to His heart and to Jesus as the true north, a great returning to Him in purity, holiness, and humility so that we can partner with all He is doing. There will be a greater returning to the true Gospel message and not a "watered down" Gospel message.

So everything I am sharing in this chapter, as hard as some of it may be, is to encourage you and to give you greater insight into what's happening and to help you in your positioning before Him to run with Him in this new era.

His Tone Is Changing

There are generals in the body of Christ whom I am so thankful for and have helped me tremendously on my journey. One of those generals for me is Patricia King. I am so thankful for her life, her heart, her relationship with the Lord, her boldness, her humility, integrity, character, and her voice to the body of Christ.

I am a very big believer in accountability and journeying and processing things with others, especially when there is such a significant shift taking place in the body of Christ like there is now. I spoke with Patricia on a few things that the Lord was showing me and revealing to me about this new era, and I mentioned to her that I had seen her ministering recently and someone had shared it on Facebook Live. As I was watching her minister, she said these words: "God's tone is changing in this new era." My goodness! That was exactly what the Lord had spoken to me and I had begun to process with Him.

As she was ministering, she was using the example of asking her children when they were young to pick up their clothes off the floor of their bedroom. If she was to come back into the room the second time and the clothes were still on the floor, her voice may be a little stronger. If she was to come into the room the third or fourth time and the clothes were still on the floor, her voice would be very strong, very to the point, and could even come across hard. She went onto to say, "Even though my tone has changed, my love remains the same."

I thought that was an excellent example of what I believe is taking place now with the voice of the Lord and will continue to in this new era. The "tone" of His voice is changing and it is calling His people to account.

I want you to hear this—it is *not* condemnation, for there is *no* condemnation for those in Christ Jesus (see Rom. 8:1), but it *is* correction. The Lord is bringing correction to the Church. He spoke to me many months ago that in this new era, the Church is going to come to a place of seeing and understanding the correction of God in a way they haven't before.

> *My son, do not despise the Lord's discipline or be weary of his reproof, for the Lord reproves him whom he loves, as a father the son in whom he delights* (Proverbs 3:11-12 ESV).

> *My son, do not reject or take lightly the discipline of the Lord [learn from your mistakes and the testing that comes from His correction through discipline]; nor despise His rebuke. For those whom the Lord loves He corrects, even as a father corrects the son in whom he delights* (Proverbs 3:11-12 AMP).

> *My child, when the Lord God speaks to you, never take his words lightly, and never be upset when he corrects you. For the Father's discipline comes only from his passionate love and pleasure for you. Even when it seems like His correction is harsh, it's still better than any father on earth gives to his child* (Proverbs 3:11-12 TPT).

I really want to look at this for a moment. I think sometimes there can be a shying away from the correction of God and the pendulum swings too far in one direction. A clear distinction has to be made. We can always approach the Lord in boldness (see Heb. 4:16) because of what Jesus has done and paid for us at Calvary, and we know that faith pleases God (see Heb. 11:6), but there is a very real place in the heart of God where He grieves. Do we live in grace? Absolutely we do (see Eph. 2:8-9)! Have we been given that glorious gift of grace? Yes, we have, thank You, Jesus! But is the Lord always happy about what we do? No, I do not believe He is.

There is a place where we can always climb up on the lap of our heavenly Daddy and He embraces, He comforts, He encourages, and He loves, but I believe that sometimes God can be wrongly portrayed as a big fluffy teddy bear and nothing grieves Him, and this communicates a message that there's a license to do what you want, and it's all okay because we live in grace and there is no fear of God. There's a familiarity with the Lord that I believe He wants to shake up and break off His people in this new era, and He is going to do it. Is He a wonderfully good Father who loves to embrace His people and we can approach Him all the time boldly because of Jesus like I mentioned? Yes! But the awakening is coming to the Church, which we will look at more in Chapter Five, that will bring the people of God to the place on their faces before Him as He reveals Himself in greater ways.

In this new era the correction of God will come, and in some ways His tone may come across as hard. That is because He *loves* you and *loves* His Church and is calling His people into a place of truth, purity, and *alignment* with Him and what He is doing so we can partner with Him in this move of God like never before.

I remember hearing Patricia sharing about her encounter with the Lord in a prayer meeting, and she saw a double-edged sword come out of heaven. When she saw it come out of heaven, it pierced into the earth, and she heard the Lord, say, *"This is My sword of truth."* As she gazed upon it, she noticed it was a two-edged sword, and the Spirit said, "This is My kindness and severity" (see Rom. 11:22). That is the perfect articulation of what I saw in an encounter with the Lord that I had. He spoke to me that in this new era there will be greater demonstrations of the Church being held to account for actions, sins, complacency, and familiarity. We are going to see a greater revelation and demonstration of Hebrews 4:12:

> *For the word of God is alive and powerful. It is sharper than the sharpest two-edged sword, cutting between soul and spirit, between joint and marrow. It exposes our innermost thoughts and desires* (NLT).

There is a deeper place when the body of Christ comes into the place of the "dealings of the Lord." When embraced, it will produce greater fruit, maturity, and integrity. The Lord has been speaking to me over and over again and saying these very words: *"I will not tolerate the games being played in the Church anymore. I have weighed the Church and found it wanting."*

Jesus Turned the Tables

Those words reminded me of a dream that I had in 2019, and I saw Jesus walk into the temple courts and begin to turn the tables over. As I was waking, He spoke: *"In this new era, I am turning over the tables. I am removing trading floors of impurity in My Church."*

> *When they arrived back in Jerusalem, Jesus entered the Temple and began to drive out the people buying and selling animals for sacrifices. He knocked over the tables of the money changers and the chairs of those selling doves, and he stopped everyone from using the Temple as a marketplace. He said to them, "The Scriptures declare, 'My Temple will be*

*called a house of prayer for all nations,' but you have turned
it into a den of thieves"* (Mark 11:15-17 NLT).

My heart was gripped. Gripped with grief in feeling the grief of
the heart of God over what He sees happening in His Church. When
Jesus overturned those tables, it was a cleansing of the temple. I was
gripped with this thought of ways that Jesus has been portrayed in the
Church as the "God who tolerates" and never angers. This has fostered
a familiarity and complacency with Him. The place of manipulating
and misusing the anointing. The place of prostituting the anointing
and the voice and revelation of God for personal gain, agenda, fame,
and influence. My heart was so grieved.

I saw a quote being shared on Instagram recently that said, "Seek
a relationship with God, instead of only using Him as a resource." My
goodness, how that aligned with the message burning within me for
this hour.

*The Lord is compassionate and gracious, **slow** to anger and
abounding in lovingkindness* (Psalm 103:8 NASB).

The Lord *is* compassionate, He is a God of grace, and He is *slow* to
anger, but He still gets angry. I believe right now there has been a lot of
"game playing" and sin in the Church that has grieved the heart of the
Lord, and He is coming to deal with these areas in the Church.

That cleansing is upon us now. Harvest is coming. A mighty outpouring is coming, but *first* the cleansing must come. The Lord is
already moving, revival fires are burning in different places, the Spirit
of God is beginning to move, but this is a very somber moment in
the body of Christ right now. The degree to which we embrace the
cleansing and purging upon the Church will be the degree to which
we run with Him in what He is going to do in the earth. That is not

the Lord dictating who will run with Him and who won't; He wants all to run with Him. It's dependent upon how much we embrace the fire of cleansing and purification that He is bringing. Embracing the purging, embracing His fire and His correction brings us deeper into intimacy with Jesus. It's a personal revival that's upon those who embrace what He is doing to cause a deeper yielding and devotion to Jesus. To be all consumed, overcome, and in love with Him at a level never walked in before.

I had a very clear dream in January of 2020, and in the dream I saw a bride and she was caught in *very* dirty and murky and mucky water. There was a coffin in the water and I heard a voice in the dream tell me that the person in the coffin, his name was Jordan. Instantly the knowing came to me that it was the Jordan River. The bride in the dream was wading through this water and as she looked up she saw a car on the water. Like Jesus walked on water, there was a car waiting on the water. In the Spirit I could feel such a strong invitation from the heart of God to *come out* of that dirty, mucky, sludgy water and to get into the car. There was a significant difference in the levels—the bride was very low down in this water sludge, and the car was way up on the water. So for the bride to get into the car it took strength to lift herself up out of the water and into the car. As the bride got into the car in the dream, the driver, whom I believe represented the Holy Spirit, said, "Make sure you wash your dress and let it air out to dry," and I woke up.

The interpretation of the dream then came to me. We are in the place where we have been crossing over. We have entered into a new era, but in order for the body of Christ to come into the place of this next move of God, which will be marked with signs, wonders, miracles (shown in the car driving on the surface of the water with its wheels not even sinking), and major demonstrations of the power of God, the

Bride of Christ must come out of the places of mixture. Out of the places of sin. Out of the place of compromise. Out of the places of partnering with sin and death. There was such a strong call from the Lord in this dream to *come out*. In order to get into the car and get into the move of God, there must be a coming out—the place of repentance and turning away from anything that is not pure, holy, and of the Lord and His Word.

Part of the "coming out" of that water was to be washed with the water of the Word to allow things to air out and dry (see Eph. 5:26). It was an uncovering of those dark and hidden places to "come into the sun" (Son)—into the light and the place of healing and restoration, to be *made ready*. Your clothes, once they have been washed and dried, are *ready to wear*. In repentance, in turning away, in consecration to the Lord, in coming out and "having your house in order" and coming back into the place of intimacy and purity before the Lord, then the clothes will be ready to be worn, ready to run with the Lord in all that He is going to do in this new era.

> *Therefore, since we have these promises, dear friends, let us purify ourselves from everything that contaminates body and spirit, perfecting holiness out of reverence for God* (2 Corinthians 7:1 NIV).

The Lord wants His Church to run with Him in this new era in freedom like never before. Jesus gave it all; He died and rose again so we can be *free*. "*Therefore if the Son makes you free, you shall be free indeed*" (John 8:36). I remember the day when the Holy Spirit whispered to me, "*Many have cheapened My death by the way that they live.*"

My heart was so gripped by His words. The more I thought about it, the more it made sense. Our lives are an offering of worship to Him, all of it, every area. The choices we make and the way we live either bring Him glory or they don't. Our heart motives behind how we live, why we do things, how we do things, etc. are all giving Him glory and praise for His death and resurrection, realizing the price He paid—or they aren't. If we aren't living in holiness, purity, and character but are taking grace as a license to sin or partnering with the ways of the world intentionally then we are cheapening His death and the beautiful sacrifice (see Rom. 12:2). He gave it all so we can be free. How much more should we give our all and our lives in worship and praise to give the Son the reward that He deserves?

A Great Awakening to the Price Jesus Paid at Calvary

In this great shaking that's coming in this new era there will be a major awakening to the *price* that Jesus paid at the Cross. There will be such an awakening to the Cross. It has begun in some ways, but we haven't seen anything yet compared to the awakening to the Gospel *in the Church* that is coming. The Gospel is being spread far and wide in the earth and many unbelievers are coming to know Jesus and finding salvation (hallelujah!), but as the Lord spoke to me: *"The Church needs to be evangelized again in many ways."*

The Church needs a great awakening to the price that was paid by our beautiful Jesus so we could have eternal life, abundant life, and run with *freedom*. The days of cheapening the death and resurrection of Jesus by taking grace as a license to sin or partnering with the ways of the world are over. The loving correction of God is coming swiftly to cause those who embrace it to run in *freedom* and *empowerment* of the Holy Spirit like never before. The Church will be awakened in a greater way to the cost of following Jesus in this new era. It isn't from the place of an orphan mentality that focuses on *what it costs*, but I believe the Lord is going to shake the Church up in a glorious way with the revelation of what He paid at Calvary. It was so stunning, so incredible, that it requires our entire life. Not a partially laid-down life, but a fully laid-down, yielded life—one that has died to self and is raised up following Christ, completely surrendered.

This new era will reveal that anointing doesn't come cheap. Yes, there's a cost, but the cost is nothing compared to the glory of knowing Him and partnering with Him to see His Kingdom extended. It will restore the fear of the Lord to the Church so that there cannot be complacency, familiarity, and game playing when it comes to following Jesus. He gave His all for us; how much more should we, from a place of deep revelation of His love and who He is, be *compelled* to give Him *everything?* I will touch more on this in the next chapter.

I want to encourage you—this is the era for the Church to *run* in what is already theirs. We are already free in Christ, we are already forgiven in Christ, we are already holy in Christ, we are already righteous in Him, but in many ways this has been head knowledge in the Church for a long time. For many now the fire of His purifying and revelation is coming to brand hearts afresh. For what you believe in your heart is what you walk in and walk out, and it is time for the Church to walk in purity, in integrity, and in the place of absolute devotion to the Lord.

This is the era of the second yes, where the Lord is calling us to lay ourselves on the altar again. This is the era when the fire of God is going to fall in intensity and where those who embrace His correction, His purifying and His alignments, will carry the fire like never before.

"You're Doing What? That's Crazy"

There is a new level of normal that the Lord is leading us into as His people. Chapter Nine is dedicated to this new level of normal in the area of faith, but I felt the prompting of the Holy Spirit to touch on this encounter I had with the Lord in the closing of this chapter.

There are going to be convictions of the Holy Spirit in this new era—a call to consecration from the Lord that is going to move you out of alignments and relationships that you may not have expected, but it is the hand of the Lord. We have already talked about the calling from the Lord to the Church to come out of sin, compromise, and mixture. There will also be a coming out of things that aren't *sin*, but are part of the call to consecration from the Lord.

There is a *going against the grain* that is going to fall upon many in this new era in greater ways. Hear me when I say this—I am not talking about going against Scripture or going out and doing crazy or goofy things. I am talking about areas of your life where the Lord will call you to be *set apart* for Him to make room for Him and to camp around His presence. It may be that He says not to walk through doors that are open; it may be that the Lord says "We are going in a different direction"; it may be a conviction to not do things or go to certain places you used to go to. I am not talking areas of sin, we have talked above about the conviction of the Lord to come out of areas of sin. What I am talking about here is a letting go and rearranging things to make room for Him to come—an even greater, intentional focus on Him.

You are setting up camp around His presence, where He is moving, and where He is leading. You may lose friends over your obedience to the Lord; you may lose favor with people, and people may look at you and say "Why are you doing that? You're crazy." You are obeying the call to consecrate yourself to the Lord by moving only where He is moving. Many may stand on the sidelines and call you religious, but you are actually moving against the grain with the Lord into new frontiers and you bow only to the fear of God and not the fear of man. I want to encourage you—if you lose friends or lose favor with man, they aren't the ones God wants surrounding you in this new era, and greater favor and friends will come to you by the hand of the Lord for the new journey. The greatest of all is that you will be known in heaven as a friend of God and one who only moves on the Word of the Lord and is not shaken by the pressures of the world or voices of man.

I know this has been a challenging chapter, but may it encourage you and be one that ignites the fire of Song of Songs 8:6-7:

> *Fasten me upon your heart as a seal of fire forevermore. This living, consuming flame will seal you as my prisoner of love. My passion is stronger than the chains of death and the grave, all consuming as the very flashes of fire from the burning heart of God. Place this fierce, unrelenting fire over your entire being. Rivers of pain and persecution will never extinguish this flame. Endless floods will be unable to quench this raging fire that burns within you. Everything will be consumed. It will stop at nothing as you yield everything to this furious fire until it won't even seem to you like a sacrifice anymore* (TPT).

Brian Simmons in his footnotes on verse 6 says this:

> The ancient Hebrew word for "seal" can also be translated "prison cell." He longs for his bride to be His love prisoner, in the prison cell of his eternal love. ...The phrase in Hebrew is "a most vehement flame" and is actually two

Hebrew words. The first is "a mighty flash of fire," and the second is "Yah," which is the sacred name for God Himself. The Hebrew *shalhebet-yah* could be translated "The Mighty Flame of the Lord Most Passionate!"

The Mighty Flame of the Lord Most Passionate! The fire of God to consume is coming and coming strongly, because He is passionately committed to seeing His Bride be His prisoner of love. Devoted completely to Him and walking in purity, in deep, deep yieldedness, completely uncompromising. How do we place this fire over our hearts? By faith. By our embrace. By our yielding to His purifying work.

Chapter Five

THE CHURCH WILL TREMBLE AGAIN

*J*still remember when the Lord spoke to me in 2019: *"I am going to cause the Church to tremble again."* I remember the incredible sense of awe and weight of His presence that came with those words. It was the resounding sound of Psalm 24:7-9 that thundered deep within me:

> *So wake up, you living gateways! Lift up your heads, you ageless doors of destiny! Welcome the King of Glory, for he is about to come through you. You ask, "Who is this Glory-King?" The Lord,*

armed and ready for battle, the Mighty One, invincible in every way! So wake up, you living gateways, and rejoice! Fling wide, you ageless doors of destiny! Here he comes; the King of Glory is ready to come in (TPT).

The Lord has been speaking to me for years about the King of Glory coming. It is time in this new era to see the King of Glory like we have never seen before. It is time to see Jesus revealed in His glory and majesty in unprecedented ways. Over and over the Lord has been speaking to me about the revelation of His majesty that is going to bring the Church to a place of decision before Him. It's a place you are summoned to, in a sense, to decide, "Am I all in or am I not?" When the Lord spoke these words, it reminded me of Jesus' words in Revelation 3:16:

So then, because you are lukewarm, and neither cold nor hot, I will vomit you out of My mouth.

The way that God is going to reveal Himself, the way that we are going to see Jesus in His majesty is going to bring the Church to a place where you must decide. As Bobby Conner says below: "God is about to reveal Himself in such a manner that He will demand our full attention."

That puts to language exactly what I feel. What we are going to see in this new era in the revelation of His majesty is going to demand all of us, our full attention. The Lord is calling us to that deep place of consecration for *"tomorrow the Lord will do wonders among you"* (Josh. 3:5).

Familiarity with God

Bobby Conner has been saying for years:

"The Church is far too familiar with a God we barely know!" But our cry for the manifest Presence of God is about to be answered (see Isaiah 64:1). Someone is at the door. Every eye shall behold His brilliance and magnificent Glory (see Isaiah 40:3-5) and every veil shall be removed in order to behold the Lamb in His Glory (see 2 Corinthians 3:18).

These are days of destiny, filled with wonder and excitement. A powerful word is coming across the entire Body of Christ—and the word is awestruck. The awe of God is returning to the people of God, filling the heart of God's people with great expectation. God is about to reveal Himself in such a manner that He will demand our full attention. Prepare to be overwhelmed, captivated, stunned and enthralled by the awareness of God.

Indeed, much will be discovered in these revelatory days concerning the Glory of God and the God of Glory. Now is the time for every child of God to behold the Lord Jesus in His revealed Glory (see John 1:14). The Word of God plainly declares that the entire earth will be filled with the knowledge of the Glory of God:

For the earth will be filled
With the knowledge of the glory of the Lord,
As the waters cover the sea.
—Habakkuk 2:14[1]

These are the days when the glory of the Lord is going to be revealed. These are the days when the Church is going to encounter the Lord and see Him "high and lifted up." These are the days when the manifest presence of God is going to come in such a mighty way it is going to leave the Church completely reformed.

The more and more I have sought the Lord regarding the restoration of the fear of the Lord in the Church, the more I have had this deep sense that we are in for gloriously wonderful days of seeing His power in signs, wonders, and miracles and greater demonstrations of Habakkuk 1:5:

> *Look around [you, Habakkuk, replied the Lord] among the nations and see! And be astonished! Astounded! For I am putting into effect a work in your days [such] that you would not believe it if it were told you* (AMPC).

The fruit of the era of the fear of the Lord being restored to the Church is going to be a people who are burning in wholehearted devotion to Him. Those who adore Jesus and walk in purity and holiness carry the light and love of God and represent Him well in the earth.

What I want to communicate clearly as we move into this chapter is the restoration of the fear of God is coming *because of His love* and *to align us* correctly with Him, His nature, His Word, and His truth *so that* we can walk in all He has for us and see the name of Jesus lifted high in the earth.

The Lord showed me that the way that His majesty and glory is going to be revealed in the Church in this new era is going to cause *one of two extremes*. It is going to cause the people of God to run to the altar and cry out for the fire of God to fall and prepare and purify, or it will cause others to run in the opposite direction in fear. Is the latter option the Lord's heart? Obviously not, but the call upon the Church is intensifying—to lay it all down, to run after Him wholeheartedly, to embrace Him and all that He is and to be living yielded to Him and

His ways. The Lord is not going to tolerate the sin and mixture that is polluting the Church and hindering her from taking her rightful place in the earth.

Sadly, there is going to be a greater demonstration of Matthew 24:12 in the body of Christ in more ways than we have seen.

> *And because lawlessness will be increased, the love of many will grow cold* (ESV).

> *There will be such an increase of sin and lawlessness that those whose hearts once burned with passion for God and others will grow cold* (TPT).

The Lord's heart is for His people to live close to Him, to be friends of God, living in the place of continual revelation of His goodness, His kindness, and His love. The place of such deep intimacy with Him and knowing His ways, living in deep reverence and awe of who He is.

There are so many Scriptures that give us wisdom and understanding on the fear of the Lord. Let's look at a few:

> *And to man He said "Behold, the fear of the Lord, that is wisdom; and to depart from evil is understanding"* (Job 28:28).

> *The fear of the Lord is the beginning of wisdom; a good understanding having all those who do His commandments; His praise endures forever* (Psalm 111:10).

> *The fear of the Lord is a fountain of life, to turn one away from the snares of death* (Proverbs 14:27).

> *In the fear of the Lord there is strong confidence, and His children will have a place of refuge* (Proverbs 14:26).

Then you will understand the fear of the Lord and find the knowledge of God (Proverbs 2:5).

Praise the Lord! Blessed is the man who fears the Lord, who delights greatly in His commandments (Psalm 112:1).

Blessed is every one who fears the Lord, who walks in His ways (Psalm 128:1).

The fear of the Lord is to hate evil, pride and arrogance and the evil way and the perverse mouth I hate (Proverbs 8:13).

And Moses said to the people "Do not fear; for God has come to test you, and that His fear may be before you, so that you may not sin" (Exodus 20:20).

Come, you children, listen to me; I will teach you the fear of the Lord (Psalm 34:11).

And He will be the stability of your times, a wealth of salvation, wisdom and knowledge; the fear of the Lord is his treasure (Isaiah 33:6 NASB).

The fear of the Lord leads to life, so that one may sleep satisfied, untouched by evil (Proverbs 19:23 NASB).

Now these are just some of the Scriptures on the fear of the Lord. Why do I include these here? Because for so long in the Church many hear the words *fear of God* and can see it as something scary. The fear of the Lord is recognizing who He is and His nature and giving Him the respect, honor, and awe due to Him.

So if there is a familiarity and a complacency in the Church toward who God is, then what is the most loving thing the Lord could do? Reveal His awe and wonder, bring a shaking to awaken His people to who He is to break that familiarity and complacency and see His people then walk in the abundant life that He purchased for them (see

John 10:10) and be actively moving with Him in the greatest move of the Spirit of God upon the earth. We have to be people who are *fully awake* to the *privilege* that it is to know Him and make Him known.

Living in the fear of God is the place of safety, the place of life. It's the place where you live in divine wisdom, in understanding, and you stay away from evil because you are so overtaken, consumed, and full of the revelation of His goodness, His love, His holiness and majesty that you live your life every day before Him as a gift to offer to Him in worship. To those you love deeply, you want to give them the best gift.

The Unexpected Uncovering

I have had quite a few encounters with the Lord over the last year where He has shown me the uncovering that is coming. There is a mighty uncovering of sin that is going to increase in the Church in this new era. It is going to be one of the ways that the fear of God is restored to the Church. I had this encounter with the Lord recently, and He showed me that there will be *unexpected uncoverings*. These unexpected uncoverings are going to come in the most unexpected places. There are some places where there is sin, where there is mixture, where there is rebellion in the Church that has been hidden for a long time. This is the era when the Lord is going to uncover those things.

In the midst of this encounter, I heard His thundering voice, and the words I heard were: *"In the uncovering the revelation will be released into the Church that I am the God who sees."* In that moment, I felt the weight of this era again. I felt the weight of His love to purify. The atmosphere that surrounded me was one of "nothing is hidden from Him." Now, I want to explain this. Hebrews 4:13-15 says:

> *And no creature is hidden from his sight, but all are naked and exposed to the eyes of him to whom we must give*

account. Since then we have a great high priest who has passed through the heavens, Jesus, the Son of God, let us hold fast our confession. For we do not have a high priest who is unable to sympathize with our weaknesses, but one who in every respect has been tempted as we are, yet without sin (ESV).

There is not one person who can hide their thoughts from God, for nothing that we do remains a secret, and nothing created is concealed, but everything is exposed and defenseless before his eyes, to whom we must render an account. So then, we must cling in faith to all we know to be true. For we have a magnificent King-Priest, Jesus Christ, the Son of God, who rose into the heavenly realm for us, and now sympathizes with us in our frailty. He understands humanity, for as a Man, our magnificent King-Priest was tempted in every way just as we are, and conquered sin (TPT).

So nothing is hidden from Him, nothing we do remains a secret, and we must give an account. But we have our beautiful Jesus who is our High Priest and is able to sympathize with our weaknesses. So we keep faith and comfort in that place that He has in every respect been tempted as we are, yet He was without sin.

In this new era in the restoration of the fear of the Lord, the uncovering is going to be threefold:

1. There will be a purifying and exposing in hearts of impure motives, areas of sin, and areas that were not recognized by the believer. The Lord will call forth repentance, and in that place there will be those who will hold to faith that Jesus is our High Priest and understands what we have walked through. They will

walk in the fear of God and embrace the fire of His Spirit to purge.

2. There will then be an exposing of sin that has been *intentional* and the sin of *rebellion*. The Holy Spirit has been convicting and drawing His people and leaders into the place of repentance and holiness, and there has been a refusal to yield to Him and His ways. In this area, there will be quite severe dealings of the Lord. When this happens, what the body of Christ *must* remember is that even when the Lord deals in severity and His tone changes, His love *doesn't* and *that* we must remember when we see the dealings of God.

3. There is going to be an exposing of wolves in sheep's clothing. *"Beware of false prophets, who come to you in sheep's clothing, but inwardly they are ravenous wolves"* (Matt. 7:15). Broken trust will come as some find they put their trust in those they thought were walking with the Lord and weren't. The Holy Spirit will heal these hearts who will be affected by the uncovering.

Coupled with the uncovering that will take place will be the healing of the Holy Spirit for those whose hearts are and were affected by the sin, the wolves, and the rebellion that those they were associated with walked in.

Unexpected uncoverings are going to take place in this new era. The hand of the Lord will bring this to purify, uproot, and align His Church to carry the greater glory. The *fruit* of the dealings of God in these areas is going to restore the fear of God to the Church. It will indeed cause the Church to tremble again at the holiness of God and the severity of sin in the eyes of the Lord. It will bring the Church to the place of repentance and awe and wonder of who He is, His majesty and glory. The burning fire of conviction will fall and increase in and upon many hearts to give all they have to Him so Jesus receives the reward He deserves.

A Warning in the Uncovering

I heard the Lord speak a strong warning in the uncovering over the body of Christ. As this uncovering takes place, this isn't a place to stand on the sidelines throwing rocks. As this uncovering continues, this is the place where the body of Christ needs to walk in love and honor.

The Lord showed me that in the uncovering, not only is He going to deal with sin, wolves in sheep's clothing, and intentional rebellion, He is going to deal with the areas of judgment in the heart of believers, He is going to deal with poisonous words and pride.

The Lord is going to remind the Church again that He corrects, His exposes, and He uncovers not to *condemn* but out of His love and to bring the Church into greater alignment. Everything He uncovers, everything He corrects, He offers repentance and redemption.

There will be some very strong dealings of the Lord in this new era upon intentional sin and rebellion, but some of these strong dealings will be the result of a lack of repentance even in the uncovering. When the Lord dealt with such things in Acts 5 and numerous times in the Old Testament, it was the result of people not walking in repentance.

Do Not Be Prideful in Purity

In the uncovering that will take place, I heard the Holy Spirit speak over the Church: *"Do not be prideful in purity."*

If you stand before the Lord in purity knowing there are no areas of your heart that the Lord has convicted you of and no areas that the Lord has told you to deal with and you haven't, guard your heart by *praying for those to whom the uncovering is happening.*

> *Judge not, that you be not judged. For with the judgment you judge, you will be judged; and with the measure you use, it will be measured back to you* (Matthew 7:1-2).

This is the call to pray.

This is the call to love.

This is the call to speak life.

Do not allow your words to be words of poison and accusation against someone whom the Lord uncovers with intentional sin or rebellion in their life. Love them through your words, your kindness, and your prayers. For as much as the Lord will hold them to account for their intentional sin, the Lord holds the Church to account for the way that they respond to these uncoverings.

These uncoverings are really going to bring forth a maturing in the body of Christ. They are going to reveal those who live close to His heart and those who are friends with God, *carrying* His heart when others fall into sin or rebellion. There will be a testing of the heart that will come upon the Church in these uncoverings that will reveal what is in the heart of God's people. That will be the place where the cry for the fire of God to come and burn up any judgment or accusation needs to happen. That's the place where the cry to love like Jesus needs to happen.

The heart of God in these uncoverings is to bring restoration and humility, but that is not just for those who have fallen. It is for the body of Christ in general to be ones who walk in love, humility, discernment, and speak words of life.

Ichabod

The last few years, God has been speaking to me about the restoration of the fear of the Lord, and since we have crossed over into this new era it has majorly increased. The Lord keeps bringing me to Scriptures over and over again regarding the fear of God and the call to live in that place of obedience to Him.

Quite a number of months ago, I was sitting with the Lord having a coffee, seeking His heart for what He wanted to speak to me about, and He spoke a word loudly: *"Ichabod."*

That was not the word I was expecting to hear. I went straight to Scripture and began reading to see what the Lord was saying. I believe this is a weighty warning to leadership in this new era and also to the body of Christ in their stewardship. So I want you to come on the journey with me into First Samuel 2:12-26:

> *Eli's sons were good for nothing. They didn't honor the Lord. When any of the people came to offer a sacrifice, here is what the priests would do. While the meat was being boiled, the servant of the priest would come with a large fork in his hand. He would stick the fork into the pan or pot or small or large kettle. Then the priest would take for himself everything the fork brought up. That's how Eli's sons treated all the Israelites who came to Shiloh. Even before the fat was burned, the priest's servant would come over. He would speak to the person who was offering the sacrifice. He would say, "Give the priest some meat to cook. He won't accept boiled meat from you. He'll only accept raw meat."*

Sometimes the person would say to him, "Let the fat be burned first. Then take what you want." But the servant would answer, "No. Hand it over right now. If you don't, I'll take it away from you by force."

That sin of Eli's sons was very great in the Lord's sight. That's because they were not treating his offering with respect.

But the boy Samuel served the Lord. He wore a sacred linen apron. Each year his mother made him a little robe. She took it to him when she went up to Shiloh with her husband. She did it when her husband went to offer the yearly sacrifice. Eli would bless Elkanah and his wife. He would say, "May the Lord give you children by this woman. May they take the place of the boy she prayed for and gave to the Lord." Then they would go home. The Lord was gracious to Hannah. Over a period of years she had three more sons and two daughters. During that whole time the boy Samuel grew up serving the Lord.

Eli was very old. He kept hearing about everything his sons were doing to all the Israelites. He also heard how his sons were sleeping with the women who served at the entrance to the tent of meeting. So Eli said to his sons, "Why are you doing these things? All the people are telling me about the evil things you are doing. No, my sons. The report I hear isn't good. And it's spreading among the Lord's people. If a person sins against someone else, God can help that sinner. But if anyone sins against the Lord, who can help them?" In spite of what their father Eli said, his sons didn't pay any attention to his warning. That's because the Lord had already decided to put them to death.

The boy Samuel continued to grow stronger. He also became more and more pleasing to the Lord and to people (NIRV).

So first, here we see that Eli's sons were living in the place of intentional sin and they were making fun of the offering to the Lord. It's very clear to see in this passage that they were not living in the fear of the Lord. So what happened? Eli rebuked them verbally in verses 23-25. They did not listen, and it says that, *"The Lord had already decided to put them to death."* That's a pretty big consequence for sin in the house of God, isn't it?

But then move to First Samuel 3. Samuel had an encounter with God and the Lord told him His plans for the sins of Eli's sons. In verse 13, God said to Samuel:

And I declare to him that I am about to punish his house forever, for the iniquity that he knew, because his sons were blaspheming God, and he did not restrain them (1 Samuel 3:13 ESV).

I want to stop here for a second. I believe that in this new era when the fear of the Lord is restored to the Church, the Lord is going to begin dealing with leaders who do not follow Scripture in the appropriate and proper ways to deal with intentional sin and rebellion in the house of God and who have turned a blind eye to it or swept it under the carpet. I remember an encounter I had where I heard the Lord's voice; He was so grieved, and He said, *"Many of the watchmen have turned a blind eye to the sin that has been in the house."* How my heart grieved over hearing the Lord say that. Instantly, I felt the fear of the Lord, I felt the love of the Lord, I felt the heart of the Lord for His Church to walk in holiness and walk in *all* that He has for them and to be the pure, spotless bride that He gave everything to redeem. It also brought me to invite the Holy Spirit to have His way in my life, to continue to create in me a heart that would always see, hear, obey, and speak when He moves.

Jochebed

On this whole revelation of leaders, watchmen, and "parenting" in the house of God, I want to share something the Lord spoke to me. When God surprised me with the word *Ichabod,* a few hours later He spoke another word—*Jochebed.* Who was Jochebed?

> *The name of Amram's wife was Jochebed the daughter of Levi, who was born to Levi in Egypt. And she bore to Amram Aaron and Moses and Miriam their sister* (Numbers 26:59 ESV).

> *When she could hide him no longer, she took for him a basket made of bulrushes and daubed it with bitumen and pitch. She put the child in it and placed it among the reeds by the river bank. And his sister stood at a distance to know what would be done to him. Now the daughter of Pharaoh came down to bathe at the river, while her young women walked beside the river. She saw the basket among the reeds and sent her servant woman, and she took it. When she opened it, she saw the child, and behold, the baby was crying. She took pity on him and said, "This is one of the Hebrews' children* (Exodus 2:3-6 ESV).

I believe that the Lord used the name *Jochebed* as an example alongside the word *Ichabod* because they both have to do with the responsibility of parenting and they both have the theme of the fear of the Lord. One story tells of what can happen when the fear of the Lord isn't being walked in and sin enters the house, and the other story tells of a woman who walked in the fear of God. I believe that God wants to encourage us. In this new era of embracing the move of His Spirit and His purging, correcting, and restoring of the fear of God to the Church, there will be even more Jochebeds who will arise who cover, entrust, and raise godly "children" in the body of Christ who will go on to do great things for the Lord. (Aaron became a priest, Miriam a prophetess, and Moses a deliverer.)

I want to honor the great mothers and fathers who have gone before in the Church. In many ways there has been a great spiritual parenting, but in others there has been a great lack that the Lord has seen. This is going to change. There is going to be a greater spiritual mothering and fathering that is going to take place in this new era as a fruit of the fear of God being restored to the Church that will bring the body into greater maturity.

Then we go on to First Samuel 4. I want you to read this whole passage.

> *And Samuel's word came to all Israel.*
>
> *Now the Israelites went out to fight against the Philistines. The Israelites camped at Ebenezer, and the Philistines at Aphek. The Philistines deployed their forces to meet Israel, and as the battle spread, Israel was defeated by the Philistines, who killed about four thousand of them on the battlefield. When the soldiers returned to camp, the elders of Israel asked, "Why did the Lord bring defeat on us today before the Philistines? Let us bring the ark of the Lord's covenant from Shiloh, so that he may go with us and save us from the hand of our enemies."*

So the people sent men to Shiloh, and they brought back the ark of the covenant of the Lord Almighty, who is enthroned between the cherubim. And Eli's two sons, Hophni and Phinehas, were there with the ark of the covenant of God.

When the ark of the Lord's covenant came into the camp, all Israel raised such a great shout that the ground shook. Hearing the uproar, the Philistines asked, "What's all this shouting in the Hebrew camp?"

When they learned that the ark of the Lord had come into the camp, the Philistines were afraid. "A god has come into the camp," they said. "Oh no! Nothing like this has happened before. We're doomed! Who will deliver us from the hand of these mighty gods? They are the gods who struck the Egyptians with all kinds of plagues in the wilderness. Be strong, Philistines! Be men, or you will be subject to the Hebrews, as they have been to you. Be men, and fight!"

So the Philistines fought, and the Israelites were defeated and every man fled to his tent. The slaughter was very great; Israel lost thirty thousand foot soldiers. The ark of God was captured, and Eli's two sons, Hophni and Phinehas, died.

That same day a Benjamite ran from the battle line and went to Shiloh with his clothes torn and dust on his head. When he arrived, there was Eli sitting on his chair by the side of the road, watching, because his heart feared for the ark of God. When the man entered the town and told what had happened, the whole town sent up a cry.

Eli heard the outcry and asked, "What is the meaning of this uproar?"

The man hurried over to Eli, who was ninety-eight years old and whose eyes had failed so that he could not see. He told Eli, "I have just come from the battle line; I fled from it this very day."

Eli asked, "What happened, my son?"

The man who brought the news replied, "Israel fled before the Philistines, and the army has suffered heavy losses. Also your two sons, Hophni and Phinehas, are dead, and the ark of God has been captured."

When he mentioned the ark of God, Eli fell backward off his chair by the side of the gate. His neck was broken and he died, for he was an old man, and he was heavy. He had led Israel forty years.

His daughter-in-law, the wife of Phinehas, was pregnant and near the time of delivery. When she heard the news that the ark of God had been captured and that her father-in-law and her husband were dead, she went into labor and gave birth, but was overcome by her labor pains. As she was dying, the women attending her said, "Don't despair; you have given birth to a son." But she did not respond or pay any attention.

She named the boy Ichabod, saying, "The Glory has departed from Israel"—because of the capture of the ark of God and the deaths of her father-in-law and her husband. She said, "The Glory has departed from Israel, for the ark of God has been captured" (1 Samuel 4 NIV).

So here we have both of Eli's sons dying in the battle with the Philistines, who take away the Ark of the Covenant from Israel. Eli falls backward off his chair and Phinehas' wife, who is pregnant, goes into labor and gives birth to a son. What does she name her son? *Ichabod*—"The Glory has departed from Israel."

The glory departed from Israel. What a scary thought. It is a terrible thing to experience the loss of the glory of God.

I believe the Lord is using these stories to bring forth a warning to us as we move in this era of unprecedented demonstrations of His power and His glory. We need to be people who walk in the fear of the Lord and recognize that the Lord takes sin very seriously. So seriously that He gave His one and only Son to die so that we could be free from its entanglements and death.

Let us never be churches that have lost the glory of the Lord, whether knowingly or unknowingly. We must never take the glory of God in our midst for granted and become complacent with sin, disobedience, and idolatry.

The Greatest Move of His Spirit Upon the Earth

You may be wondering why I would include these stories in this chapter or even end this chapter this way.

Because we are in a somber moment. God is preparing us for the greatest move of His Spirit upon the earth, and it isn't all "sunshine and lollipops." We need words like this from Scripture to confront us and challenge us and take us deeper in Him.

As the Lord spoke to me: *"The game-playing days in the Church are over."* This chapter is one of the major warnings God has given me for this new era. The toleration of sin, rebellion, idol worship, complacency, and half-hearted obedience is being dealt with in the Church. I believe there is a strong warning from the heart of God upon us as the Church right now in this new era.

We have entered the time of the greatest demonstration of the glory of God being revealed in the Church that we have ever seen. The fear of God being restored to the Church. The era when the Church is going to rise up and walk in her authority and in faith like never before, seeing the most spectacular signs, wonders, and miracles that have ever been seen. The time when the harvest of souls is going to be greater than we could ever imagine. When our beautiful Jesus is going to be seen high and lifted up and His goodness spread across the whole earth. Culture transformed. Revival and reformation in the Church; transformation in the earth. The Isaiah 60 time: "Arise and shine for your light has come." The era of the Church seeing the impossible become possible. The era when the Church sees greater things done than Jesus did when He walked the earth (see John 14:12-14); when Jesus receives His full reward. Habakkuk 2:14 exploding, that the whole earth may know the name of Jesus and know His glory, His love, and His goodness. Oh, that the whole earth may know John 3:16 and the extravagant love of the Father that sent His one and only Son that whoever believes in Him shall not perish but receive everlasting life. The great outpouring of His Spirit that is ahead is more glorious than we know.

In Acts 5 is the story of Ananias and Sapphira, who lied to the Church and the Holy Spirit and were struck dead for it. The Scripture says:

> So great fear came upon all the church and upon all who heard these things (Acts 5:11).

Then you go on to read the rest of the book of Acts and you see great signs, wonders, and miracles occurring.

God is preparing His people. Out of His love, He is aligning His people to carry what He is going to release. He is issuing the warning as the preparation for the greatest move of the Spirit of God in the Church and earth that we have ever seen. We must embrace it through our love and devotion to Jesus, our obedience to Him, and living in the place of awe and reverence before Him. Because we live in the place of tenderness and encounter with Him daily and in His Word, we are living out of the overflow of the revelation of His nature and holiness and sacrifice He paid for us at Calvary. He gave everything when I didn't deserve it. What love is this! I give my all to the King of kings and Lord of lords!

Embrace the shaking that's coming; the fruit of it is glorious—to see Him like in Isaiah 6 and to live in the place of blessing, wisdom, and life rooted in the fear of the Lord.

May we not be found with "Ichabod" written over our lives.

Note

1. Bobby Conner, "Awestruck by What We Behold!" August 21, 2014, bobbyconner.org, accessed April 15, 2020, https://www .bobbyconner.org/articles/Awestruck-by-What-We-Behold!

Chapter Six

BACK TO SCHOOL WITH THE HOLY SPIRIT: I HEARD HIM SAY "THE KEY IS HUMILITY"

know I have said and will continue to say this numerous times in this book, because it is really what I believe the overall invitation of this book is—*know His ways*. A few months into 2019, as I was sitting with Jesus having a coffee, the Lord whispered these words to me: *"Back to school with the Holy Spirit."* The sense that surrounded me strongly was not to *assume anything* in this new era. Yes, we know the Lord; yes, we have a history with God; yes, we know His nature and we have encountered His heart, heard His voice, and learned of His ways and the journey of discovering Him is glorious. But as we have entered this new era, we cannot look to what God did yesterday as the road map for what He is going to do today.

I remember recently hearing my friend Todd Weatherly saying, "Many in the body of Christ have become familiar with a God that they don't know." The call in this new era is to really know the Lord deeply and to know His ways. As I have sought His heart on how to be ready and positioned for what He is going to do, the Lord showed me the *key* for this new era and walking in all that He has for us. Do you know what it was?

Humility!

There is a completely new road map and it requires the people of God to be in the place of humility before Him to walk in all that He has for them. I felt strongly that the Lord wanted me to include this chapter here because humility *is* the key to partnering with Him in all He is going to do in this new era and it is the key to stewarding all that He is and will release.

> At that time the disciples came to Jesus, saying, "Who is the greatest in the kingdom of heaven?" And calling to him a child, he put him in the midst of them and said, "Truly, I say to you, unless you turn and become like children, you will never enter the kingdom of heaven. Whoever humbles himself like this child is the greatest in the kingdom of heaven" (Matthew 18:1-4 ESV).
>
> At that time the disciples came to ask Jesus, "Who is considered to be the greatest in heaven's kingdom realm?" Jesus called a little one to his side and said to them, "Learn this

*well: Unless you **dramatically change your way of thinking** and **become teachable,** and learn about heaven's kingdom realm with the wide-eyed wonder of a child, you will never be able to enter in. Whoever continually humbles himself to become like this gentle child is the greatest one in heaven's kingdom realm"* (Matthew 18:1-4 TPT).

I love Brian Simmons' commentary notes on this Scripture. In verse 1 the disciples ask Jesus: *"Who is considered to be the greatest in heaven's kingdom realm?"* Brian shares, "The Aramaic is 'Who will reign in the kingdom realm of heaven?'" And in verse 4 on the words *"humbles himself,"* Brian states this means "to see yourself as unimportant in your own eyes."

This is not a place of seeing ourselves as "unworthy" or "I am a worm" or "I am nothing." It is living in a place of revelation of who we are in Christ and not living in a place of pride. It is living in the revelatory recognition that "I am who I am because of Him." It's not living in false humility; it's about recognizing His glory, His nature, His majesty, and His beauty and living in light of who He is. It's not the focus upon "self" and living from insecurity, wounding, or "look who I am and look how important I am." I love what Bill Johnson says:

> In my own pursuit of God, I often became preoccupied with ME! It was easy to think that being constantly aware of my faults and weakness was humility. It's not! If I'm the main subject, talking incessantly about my weaknesses, I have entered into the most subtle form of pride.[1]

Humility is not criticizing yourself. Humility is not thinking of yourself less than who He says you are or being weak. Humility is living in the place where *He* is the main focus and being teachable and finding strength and confidence in Him.

I love how Kris Vallotton defines humility: "Humility is not demeaning ourselves but exalting our God."[2] I find these words so powerful, because the Lord showed me in this new era those who will truly carry this next move of God and *reign* in the earth, walking in their authority, will be those who are positioned before the Lord in the place of surrender and walking in humility.

In this new era, the Lord is really going to deal with pride in the hearts of believers. There is a purification that has begun in the Church, and it is going to continue in significant ways. The purifying fire of the Lord is falling upon the Church and is going to continue to increase in intensity in this new era. The Lord is going to expose the areas of pride within hearts and the area of self-promotion and impurity of the heart. We know that there is no condemnation for those in Christ Jesus (see Rom. 8:1). So the exposing of those areas of the heart will not be to condemn but to purge, to purify, to correct. The purifying fire of the Lord will fall heavily in this new era to expose the impurity of the heart and call forth repentance.

Now, I want to take you on a little adventure into a dream I had last year. You may start to read this dream and think, "Lana, what in the world does this have to do with humility?" Stay with me, you will see.

Children Are Key in This New Era

At the start of last year, I had a dream in which the Lord spoke to me concerning this new era. He spoke in my dream: *"Lana, it will not begin until it begins with the children."* Since this dream, the Lord has been speaking to me in many different ways about how He is going to move and reveal Himself through children in this new era.

What He is going to do through children is going to astound, confound, and shock the Church like never before. There will be mighty, unprecedented demonstrations of the power of God through children in this new era. The signs, wonders, and miracles that will flow through children will be incredible; even some miracles that the Church has never seen will be demonstrated through children.

The Lord showed me that this mighty move of the Spirit of God through children will offend the religious mindset and pride in the heart. This is one of the many ways that the Lord is going to expose areas of the religious spirit and the spirit of pride in the hearts of believers.

The Lord showed me there may be a temptation from old wine-skins or mentalities to "overlook" the children or push the children aside. I heard Him say, *"Do not push the children aside in this new era."* In this new era, there are going to be incredible demonstrations of the Lord's power and glory. He is going to reveal Himself in such profound ways that it is going to leave the people of God and the world in awe and wonder of who He is. The Lord is going to reintroduce the Church and the world to His power and one of the ways He is going to do that is the way He is going to move through the children. I heard the Lord say:

"Children will come to the forefront in this new era in the ways that they will display My power, My voice, My glory, and My Word. There is going to be a powerful move of My Spirit amongst the children, and if you do not have eyes to see and ears to hear, you will be offended by My move through the children in this new era.

There will be greater increase in divine revelation, wisdom, and insight being released through the children. 'Out of the mouths of babes' will become more and more normal in this new era, and it will take humility to receive what I am saying and doing when I release it through a child. My voice through the children in this new era will leave many in awe of Me" (see Matt. 21:16; Ps. 8:2). "Watch My prophetic voice **resound loudly** in this new era through the children. Through the mouths of children will be one of the ways I will herald greater revelation of the times and seasons."

The enemy has been attacking the family unit and children because of what God is doing and going to do through them. Matthew 11:25 will be demonstrated significantly in this new era:

> At that time Jesus declared, "I thank you, Father, Lord of heaven and earth, that you have hidden these things from the wise and understanding and revealed them to little children" (ESV).

The Lord is going to release His wisdom through the children and to those who are walking in humility and childlike faith. I heard the Lord say: *"Pay attention to the children in gatherings. Do not overlook them or push them aside."* In meetings, in homes, in conferences, in churches—pay attention to what the Lord is saying and doing in the children, for in them the Lord is going to reveal profound, divine insight. In many places, the children will release the fire of God and the move of His Spirit in *powerful* ways. Those with eyes to see and ears to hear will hear His voice and see the move of His Spirit through the children.

There will be a major increase in significant breakthrough and healing by the Holy Spirit moving through children in this new era.

People will receive life-changing, significant breakthrough, healing, and divine direction through children. There will be an even greater increase of children carrying and receiving divine strategies and the Lord's answers to adults' prayers in this new era. There will be a significant increase in children seeing in the spirit and articulating what is taking place, bringing greater clarity and direction to adults. I heard the Lord say, *"Watch the wave of My healing that is going to flow through the children in this new era. The media will even be reporting more and more on the rising of gifted children and astonishing works through children, which will testify to Me, My goodness, and My hand."*

> *Jesus said, "Let the little children come to me and do not hinder them, for to such belongs the kingdom of heaven"* (Matthew 19:14 ESV).

> *Jesus overheard them and said, "I want little children to come to me, so never interfere with them when they want to come, for heaven's kingdom realm is composed of beloved ones like these! Listen to this truth: No one will enter the kingdom realm of heaven unless he becomes like one of these!" Then he laid his hands on each of them and went on his way* (Matthew 19:14-15 TPT).

I heard the Lord say:

"Include them, engage with them, embrace them, receive My divine wisdom and revelation through them. Receive My divine strategy in training them, raising them, teaching them, but also partnering with them to see My Kingdom established and My glory revealed in the earth. *It's time to see the children arise, walking in My power like never before.*"

The way the Lord is going to use children in this new era is going to be astounding. We are already seeing major demonstrations of the Lord's power and His love flowing through children. As a mother of three, of think of how many times a day my children teach me about the Lord—how they teach me about His kindness and they *teach me.* I have honestly lost count of the number of times my ten-year-old, Elijah, has prophesied to me without even realizing what He's doing. The key for me in those interactions with my kids is my ability to *receive* from my children. There are times when the Lord has corrected me and convicted me through my six-year-old, Judah, who has such a soft heart and a strong mantle of justice. If something isn't how it should be, he will tell you. When I have felt the conviction of the Holy Spirit through the raw words of my six-year-old, I have had that choice in that moment to *recognize* that the Holy Spirit is speaking to me and then *receive* it.

A Heart That Is Teachable

Humility is having a heart that's teachable and able to receive, even when what the Lord is offering to us and releasing to us comes in a package we don't expect. Whether it's my six-year-old or it's the lady down the street who really annoys you, the Lord will use different people and ways to speak to us and teach us, and sometimes the things He uses can expose areas of pride or a lack of a teachable heart.

The Lord showed me that some of the ways He is going to use children are going to expose pride, self-importance, self-promotion, and immaturity in hearts. He isn't exposing these things because He is mean or because He is not a good, kind, and loving Father; He is exposing these things because they are poison in the heart. Because of His love for us, He is so committed to develop within His people hearts of humility and purity so that we can represent Him well on the earth.

If there is any pride, self-importance, or self-promotion, then it will be a struggle to receive what the Lord does through the children in this new era. Sadly, in the Church today there is such a focus upon "platforms" and numbers of Facebook followers. Who I am having lunch, dinner, and coffee with at a conference. And let me post the photo on social media so everyone can see the famous Christian leaders *I* am friends with. If the heart motive is to self-promote or "look at me," then there's an issue.

My goodness, how this needs to be uprooted out of the Church and hearts. This is not in line with the life of Jesus. This is not in line with the words of Jesus. If anything, the very life of Jesus *exposes* the culture of the Church today as far from what He modeled. Now, I am not saying there is anything wrong with big meetings and platforms with large influence. What am I talking about is the *condition of the heart* in stewarding those platforms. There are spoken and unspoken "requirements" that have been built in the Church to define success or where the Holy Spirit is going to move and where He isn't, based upon the size of the platform.

You will see me talk often in this book about stewardship and the fire of God to purify in this new era. I will refer to it over and over. Why? Because it is a major part of what is going to take place over the next few years. The magnitude of the reformation, the magnitude of the outpouring, the magnitude of the display of His power that will be seen is *so* monumental. He is bringing radical and monumental alignment, calling the Church to be ready.

It is going to be so glorious to see the Lord move in the children in powerful ways, exposing hearts of many. The Lord has showed me that

He is also going to move in places that haven't been heard of. Some of the biggest fires of His presence will be seen in small places that have been "forgotten" and no one would have ever heard of. Faithful pastors in country towns who are seeking God with all their hearts and crying out for an outpouring of His Spirit and for the Lord to come and reveal His glory. I'm not saying the Lord isn't going to move in well-known places and larger cities. What I am saying is that there will be mighty moves of His Spirit in the most unexpected of places. Some who will carry this next move of God will be some of the most unexpected people. This will be like a divine litmus test upon the hearts of God's people in the Church—are hearts blossoming in the fruit of humility or the fruit of pride?

In this divine litmus test through the move of the Spirit in children, if the Spirit of God reveals pride, that is when we must embrace the fire of His correction and conviction and repent. The loving arms of our Father embrace us tightly in that place of repentance, and the fire of His love and purging so engulfs our hearts to make us more like Him. The danger comes in ignoring the conviction of the Holy Spirit and ignoring His correction.

> *Pride goes before destruction, and a haughty spirit before a fall. It is better to be of a lowly spirit with the poor than to divide the spoil with the proud* (Proverbs 16:18-19 ESV).

> *Your boast becomes a prophecy of a future failure. The higher you lift up yourself in pride, the harder you'll fall in disgrace. It's better to be meek and lowly and live among the poor than to live high and mighty among the rich and famous* (Proverbs 16:18-19 TPT).

Fear of the Lord

This brings me right back to a key to humility—living in the fear of the Lord, living daily in the wonder and awe of who He is. That is what fosters a heart of humility. As I live deeply in the garden with Him, close to His heart, so close that I can hear His heart beating in my ears, then I recognize when His heart skips a beat with excitement or when His heart is longing. I want to be so close that I recognize it all. I don't miss a beat. As I live in the place of constant awareness of our beautiful Jesus, seeing Him in His majesty and what He paid at Calvary, I live my life laid down in awe of who He is.

As I sit here writing this chapter and thinking about humility, I feel the invitation of His heart to come deeper and deeper still. I feel His love surround me so strongly, inviting me to know Him deeper than I have, to lay everything aside, to just be His friend. That is the answer to humility. Living close to His heart and being His friend doesn't mean I am perfect or get everything right all the time; it just means that when something creeps into my heart, I'm living so close and sensitive to His Spirit that I instantly know when something isn't right. As I move in the place of repentance, I am able to keep short accounts with the Lord. In the place of living close to Him, if there are things in my heart I wasn't aware of, things recent or things from a long time ago, I recognize it when He touches them and exposes them, and I can respond and allow Him to speak His truth and bring healing.

Now to the second part of my dream.

Childlike Faith

The Holy Spirit spoke to me that not only will there be a mighty move of the Spirit of God that is going to pour through children, there is also an invitation in this new era to *childlike faith*. God is looking for childlike faith and trust, for those who will take Him at His Word and trust Him completely like a little child. Not childlike in immaturity, but childlike in faith, trust, and wonder of who He is.

I want you to think with me for a moment about childlike faith. What is childlike faith? Let's use my kids as an example again— Elijah, Judah, and Benjamin. Now, not only does the Lord speak to me through them and they have taught me so much, these boys have taught me more about childlike faith than I ever thought possible. I cannot count how many questions they ask me a day. How inquisitive they are, how hungry they are to know, to learn, to explore. How adventurous they are in life. They come to me and ask me a question, and they live from the place of, "If Mummy said it, I believe it."

The trust comes from knowing me, knowing my character, knowing who I am, knowing my love for them, and knowing my faithfulness to them.

They know me.

So when I tell them something, they trust me. They take me at my word. They simply believe.

I believe the key to childlike faith is knowing Him, His character, and His love. Knowing His nature, I trust in *His ways*. Can it be that simple? I believe it is. When we know Him intimately and we know His heart, we know His goodness, we know He is a good and perfect Father (see Matt. 5:48), so we take Him at His Word and walk forth in complete trust and childlike faith.

Like I said above, it's not about having all the answers or getting everything perfect. It is not even about knowing what you are doing in this new era. Believe me, a lot of the time I have no idea what I'm doing; I am just seeking to be His friend, following His voice to the best of my ability, and trusting in Him to do in me and through me what He desires.

> *Trust in the Lord with all your heart, and do not lean on your own understanding. In all your ways acknowledge him, and he will make straight your paths* (Proverbs 3:5-6 ESV).

Let's look at Matthew 18:1-4 again for a moment. I want to focus on another part of this verse:

> **Learn this well:** *Unless you* **dramatically change your way of thinking** *and* **become teachable,** *and learn about heaven's kingdom realm with the wide-eyed wonder of a child, you will never be able to enter in* (Matthew 18:3 TPT).

Both of these phrases communicate "pay attention," "invest into this," "don't take this lightly." I want to pay attention to and invest into every word God speaks, especially when He says, "learn this well." As I have pondered this passage with the Lord, He has spoken to me and emphasized this passage so strongly because this is the *key* to entering the Kingdom and partnering with all God will do in the earth.

One thing I want to implore you to do in this new era is to throw your heart and soul into knowing God and learning His ways. Become teachable. If you receive nothing else from this chapter, I want you to receive this. Matthew 22:35-38 says:

> *One of them, an expert in religious law, tried to trap him with this question: "Teacher, which is the most important commandment in the law of Moses?" Jesus replied, "'You must love the Lord your God with all your heart, all your soul, and all your mind.' This is the first and greatest commandment"* (NLT).

Become an expert in one thing—*knowing Him* and *knowing His ways*. Not in a prideful way, but make that your number-one priority. In this new era, be continually positioned in the place of humility before the Lord, confessing to Him that you don't know everything and you haven't got everything worked out. You are living day by day on the revelation that He releases to you, your daily bread, and by every word that precedes out of the mouth of the Lord (see Matt. 4:4; 6:11). Live deeply in the place of intimacy, throwing *everything* you have into loving God, yielding every part of you to Him and to His love so that He would overtake you and blossom within you. *Give everything to know Him intimately.*

Do not take His words lightly. They are your life. They are your daily bread. They are the place of protection for your heart and mind. The shaking upon the Church in this new era is to bring the eyes of the Church away from "look at me and my platform" and other loves and affections of the heart, back to the gaze of Jesus, eyes locked with Him. The dance of the first love. The place of humility where a life is laid down for one thing alone—Jesus Christ. I am not here to serve myself; I am not here to get glory for me and my name. I am here to make His name great. The one thing I want to be known for when I leave this earth is how my life was used to bring glory to Him, how His name was glorified and lifted high in and through my life, so that I would be known as one who loved God with all my heart, all my soul, all my mind.

This intense, purifying fire of God is for one thing alone—to bring the Church deeper into that place. Back to the main thing—Jesus! Jesus is going to take His rightful place in the Church again, as the head (see Col. 1:18).

Back to school with the Holy Spirit:

Trust in the Lord completely, and do not rely on your own opinions. With all your heart rely on him to guide you, and he will lead you in every decision you make. Become intimate with him in whatever you do, and he will lead you wherever you go. Don't think for a moment that you know it all, for wisdom comes when you adore him with undivided devotion and avoid everything that is wrong. Then you will find the healing refreshment your body and spirit long for (Proverbs 3:5-8 TPT).

What a gloriously rich passage with keys for this new era. Take it as a bouquet of some of the Kingdom keys of wisdom from the heart of God to help you navigate this time we have entered into.

- Trust in the Lord completely.
- Don't rely on your own opinions (natural wisdom).
- With all your heart surrender and yield in humility before Him, and then you will have direction and wisdom for your decisions.
- Become intimate with Him—a friend of God.
- Don't think you know it all—become teachable and humble.
- Burn in adoration for Him with undivided devotion; love Him with all your heart, soul, mind, and strength.
- Consecrate yourself and avoid what is wrong.

Then you will find healing refreshment that your body and spirit long for.

Era of The Unexpected

The Lord spoke to me to add a prophetic word here at the end of this chapter that I released in November of 2019. This is an encouragement and reminder to us all to draw close to Him, to know His ways, be teachable, and ask for His wisdom and discernment to recognize when He moves, even if it's in ways we don't expect.

Over the last year the Lord has been speaking to me a lot about how important it will be and is in this new era to be a friend of God and living in deep intimacy with Him. To be positioned close to His heart asking Him to develop in us eyes that see, ears that hear, and a heart that discerns His ways.

He showed me that if we aren't living in that place of deep intimacy, close to His heart, postured in humility to allow the Spirit of God to school us in His ways, many would be offended at the way that God moves, who He uses, and what it looks like.

This conviction has continued to grow stronger and stronger within me over the past few months, and recently I heard the Lord speak over the body of Christ: *"Be careful not to criticize the ways I am moving in this new era."*

When the Lord spoke this, instantly the Lord highlighted the *mouth* to me again. There was such a strong sense that surrounded me: "Do not be quick to judge something as *not* God because it doesn't fit the box or paradigm that you think it should."

This is the *era of the unexpected!* This is the era when God is going to do things so out of the box, because He is wanting to reveal His majesty, His glory, His power. We have only just begun to see a "drop in the ocean" of what God is going to do in this new era. God is going to demonstrate His power, His glory, His splendor in ways that we have never seen before, but it *requires* having eyes to see and ears to hear.

Matthew 13:10-16 has been burning in me:

> *Then his disciples approached Jesus and asked, "Why do you always speak to people in these hard-to-understand parables?"*
>
> *He explained, "You've been given the intimate experience of insight into the hidden truths and mysteries of the realm of heaven's kingdom, but they have not. For everyone who listens with an open heart will receive progressively more revelation until he has more than enough. But those who don't listen with an open, teachable heart, even the understanding that they think they have will be taken from them. That's why I teach the people using parables, because they think they're looking for truth, yet because their hearts are unteachable, they never discover it. Although they will listen to me, they never fully perceive the message I speak. The prophecy of Isaiah describes them perfectly:*
>
> *"'Although they listen carefully to everything I speak, they don't understand a thing I say. They look and pretend to see, but the eyes of their hearts are closed. Their minds are dull and slow to perceive, their ears*

are plugged and are hard of hearing, and they have deliberately shut their eyes to the truth. Otherwise they would open their eyes to see, and open their ears to hear, and open their minds to understand. Then they would turn to me and let me instantly heal them.'

"But your eyes are privileged, for they see. Delighted are your ears, for they are open to hear all these things" (TPT).

The Lord is inviting the body of Christ into a place of partnering with Him in the greatest move of the Spirit of God that we have ever seen in the earth, but stewarding that move and partnering with Him requires hearts that are yielded in humility and those who are friends with God and are schooled in the ways of God.

I felt the fear of God so strongly as the Lord spoke those words to me: "Be careful not to criticize the new things that I am doing in this new era."

There is such a strong feeling in the atmosphere to "watch your mouth" in this new era like never before. Do not throw around careless words, especially being quick to deem something as "not God" because it looks different from what you have experienced or seen before.

There is a *summoning* of the Lord upon the people of God now. No matter what denomination, no matter what stream you flow in, what network you align with, there is a *summoning* from the heart of God right now into the place of intimacy, laying down opinions, preconceived ideas, judgments and expectations to *ask* the Holy Spirit to reveal His truth, to reveal His ways, and to lead us into *all* truth. This is the place of preparation for what is to come. This is the place of positioning to partner with God in what He is about to do. This is the place of stewarding this new move of His Spirit and not "standing in the way" of what God is doing.

> *But when He, the Spirit of truth, comes, He will guide you into all the truth; for He will not speak on His own initiative, but whatever He hears, He will speak; and He will disclose to you what is to come* (John 16:13 NASB).

Be in the Word

This is the time to be in the Word like never before, asking for wisdom and discernment.

The Lord is calling His people deeper into the Word of God. In this new era of acceleration, it is *imperative* that the people of God are deeper in the Word of God and knowing the Word of God more than ever. Do not allow busyness or distraction to keep you out of the Word of God. Be schooled in the ways of God in the Word as the Spirit of God illuminates truth to you. For the Lord is going to show you and confirm to you *through* the Word of God what He is doing in this new era. Even when it looks different, outside your comfort zone, paradigm, or box, the Lord is going to confirm that it's Him through His Word.

He will *not* step outside of His Word; He will not contradict His Word; He will *confirm* through His Word. The *key* is to approach the Word of God with a teachable heart of humility to allow the Holy Spirit to show you what He needs to show you, even if the way He moves offends your mindset. What He is going to do in the earth is going to be *glorious!* In the *establishing* of His Kingdom upon the earth in this new era, some things will be *dismantled*, some things will be *rearranged*, some things will be *shaken* and without eyes to see and ears to hear the temptation will be to shout *"Look what the enemy is doing"* but actually it is the *hand of God* dismantling and rearranging things that have been built on foundations that are not right or pure. It will be the hand of God that will dismantle and rearrange things that were part of the old season, and it's time for new structures, a new wineskin.

Matthew 15:5-12 has been burning on my heart. The words of Jesus:

> *"But you teach that it's permissible to say to your parents when they are in financial need, 'Whatever gift you would have received from me I can keep for myself, since I dedicated it as an offering to God.' This doesn't honor your father or mother. And you have elevated your tradition above the words of God. Frauds and hypocrites! Isaiah described you perfectly when he said: These people honor me only with their words, for their hearts are so very distant from me. They pretend to worship me, but their worship is nothing more than the empty traditions of men." Then Jesus turned to the crowd and said, "Come, listen and open your heart to understand. What truly contaminates a person is not what he puts into his mouth but what comes out of his*

mouth. That's what makes people defiled." Then his dis-
ciples approached him and said, "Don't you know that
what you just said offended the Pharisees?" (TPT)

This is a very important warning from the Lord that all of us must take on board. We *must* be in the secret place as friends of God, *knowing Him* above *all else* in this new era, and not be found to be ones throwing stones with our words at what *God* is actually doing in the earth. Let us not be found standing in the *way* of what God is doing rather than partnering *with Him* in the greatest move of the Spirit of God in the earth. The move of God in this new era is going to expose the religious spirit unlike anything we have ever seen before.

There is a separation that is taking place in the body of Christ right now by the move of God that's beginning, and it is separation that is displaying those who *know Him* intimately and have eyes to see and ears to hear and live grounded and founded in the Word of God and know His heart—and those who don't. This is going to become more and more apparent as we venture into this new era. The heart of God is that *all* would draw close and partner with Him, but it is our responsibility to be positioned in humility. In the place of humility, the Spirit of God through His Word and His truth will break deception, pride, and offense in the hearts of many as there is a drawing close to Him and humility that takes place.

A Tidal Wave

There's going to be a major tidal wave of streams coming together like never before—do not criticize it or stand in the way.

The Lord showed me streams of all denominations coming together like never before in this new era. It is going to take place in ways we have never seen. There are going to be *major* demonstrations of unity that are going to take place in this mighty move of God that will take place in the earth.

As I watched this take place, I heard the sound of "murmuring" and "bickering" in the Spirit. I heard the sound of believers criticizing, speaking against, and whispering, "We don't partner with *them*; we do not align with *them*."

This is the time to lay down offenses, to deal with anything in the heart that would hinder us from partnering with our brothers and sisters in Christ because of denominational differences or offenses. The streams are going to merge like never before and it is going to be under *one* thing—under the *name* of Jesus Christ.

In this new era, the streams will come together to build together what God is building. Do not be offended at how God does this. Do not allow offense to keep you from flowing in the tidal wave of His Spirit bringing the streams together. It's time to let go and repent of pride, offense, and bickering. It's time to ask the Holy Spirit to bring healing to the heart and greater revelation of the love of Jesus to embrace our brothers and sisters in Christ and stop throwing knives and stones at each other with our words. It's time to be people who walk in *love*. Loving one another, honoring one another, laying down our lives for our friends (see John 15:13), and considering others better than ourselves (see Phil. 2:3).

This new era will see a *greater* manifestation of John 15. The shaking in the Church by the hand of God will bring to the surface more and more things that have stood in the way of the body of Christ walking in John 15.

God is bringing purity to the Church. God is purifying the body of Christ. The Lord is returning for a pure and spotless bride (see Eph. 5:27), and in this new era the fire of God is already beginning to purify, expose, refine, and purge to *prepare* us to walk in the purity and holiness that we are called to walk in, in Christ. There will be some "upturning of the tables" by the hand of God more and more in this new era to usher in purity in the body of Christ.

Let us be people who are living deep in the secret place, knowing Him, seeing Him, being taught by Him, and learning His ways.

Let us be found not criticizing what God is doing in this new era if it looks completely different from what we expect. Let us be people who cry out, "God, make me ready! Teach me! Give me eyes that see and ears that hear to *discern* what You are doing and partner with You even if it offends my mind."

All I can say in ending here is...*Selah!*

Notes

1. Bill Johnson, *When Heaven Invades Earth* (Shippensburg, PA: Destiny Image Publishers, 2005), 147.

2. Kris Vallotton, *The Supernatural Ways of Royalty* (Shippensburg, PA: Destiny Image Publishers, 2017), 116.

Chapter Seven

I Heard the Lord Say "Ferocious in Flint-Like Focus"

The Lord continues to repeat to me over and over about the importance of *focus* in this new era. It is imperative that we as God's people are intently focused on Jesus and His Word and His assignments for this new era. The level of acceleration that is being released is really not like anything we have ever walked in, seen, or perceived.

For the past four to five years, the Lord has had me in the story of Elijah and the cloud the size of a man's hand in First

Kings 18:41-46. I have been ministering and prophesying from this passage, and the Lord has released so much encouragement to His people to remain in the place of believing, interceding, and contending for what He has spoken and revealed because "the cloud the size of a man's hand is about to rise up out of the sea." Then, for the last year, the Lord has had me focus on verse 46.

> *The power of the Lord came on Elijah and, tucking his cloak into his belt, he ran ahead of Ahab all the way to Jezreel* (1 Kings 18:46 NIV).

> *The Lord gave special strength to Elijah, He tucked his cloak into his belt and ran ahead of Ahab's chariot all the way to the entrance of Jezreel* (1 Kings 18:46 NLT).

That's where we are right now. The power of the Lord will come upon believers; supernatural acceleration will be released to run with Him and see things really speeding up by His hand and power.

Era of Acceleration

On this journey of seeking the Lord regarding this release of unprecedented acceleration, I heard the Lord say to me recently, *"Lana, the level of acceleration that I am releasing in this new era has not been walked in before."*

Those words struck me so strongly—*"has not been walked in before."* It's not like God is repeating a level of past acceleration; this is a completely new level of acceleration being released that we haven't walked in.

The Lord continued to speak:

"So if you haven't walked in this level of acceleration that I am releasing that means that you don't know how to navigate the pathway, so I am inviting My people to come close to My heart, deep in My Word, and listening to My voice so I can teach you how to navigate this new level of acceleration where you remain close to Me, deeply rooted in relationship and intimacy with Me as your first love."

Instantly I remembered an encounter I had with the Lord in 2015, from which I released a prophetic word in 2017. I am going to post this encounter here because I believe the Lord is breathing heavily upon this again right now as we have entered into this new era when there will be unprecedented acceleration.

About two years ago I had a radical encounter with the Lord that changed my life. Sitting on the floor of my prayer room delighting in Him, He began to show me a season of incredible breakthrough, blessing upon blessing, increase, and abundance that was coming to the Church. In that season of incredible provision, that season of incredible harvest and fruitful abundance, there would be *so* much blessing all around, but in the midst of all the blessing, all the provision, and all the increase, I heard Him whisper to me, *"But don't lose Me in the breakthrough. Don't forget Me."*

This incredible sense surrounded me—in the midst of the increase that was coming that was so significant, so beautiful, so refreshing, the change of the season into a land full of breakthrough of promises—to not forget Him. To be *intentional* in the blessing and abundant "new lands," to be pressing deeper into the quiet place, the secret place of intimacy with Him like never before.

Recently, this encounter has been stirring in me so much. When I asked the Lord why it was stirring in me again, He whispered to me that two years ago I was forerunning what He is releasing now.

The Lord recently brought me back to a passage of Scripture that He brought before my eyes a year ago. It's from Deuteronomy 8:7-18:

For the Lord your God is bringing you into a good land— a land with brooks, streams, and deep springs gushing out into the valleys and hills; a land with wheat and barley, vines and fig trees, pomegranates, olive oil and honey; a land where bread will not be scarce and you will lack nothing; a land where the rocks are iron and you can dig copper out of the hills.

When you have eaten and are satisfied, praise the Lord your God for the good land he has given you. Be careful that you do not forget the Lord your God, failing to observe his commands, his laws and his decrees that I am giving you this day. Otherwise, when you eat and are satisfied, when you build fine houses and settle down, and when your herds and flocks grow large and your silver and gold increase and all you have is multiplied, then your heart will become proud and you will forget the Lord your God, who brought you out of Egypt, out of the land of slavery. He led you through the vast and dreadful wilderness, that thirsty and waterless land, with its venomous snakes and scorpions. He brought you water out of hard rock. He gave you manna to eat in the wilderness, something your ancestors had never known, to humble and test you so that in the end it might go well with you. You may say to yourself, "My power and the strength of my hands have produced this wealth for me." But remember the Lord your God, for it is he who gives you the ability to produce wealth, and so confirms his covenant, which he swore to your ancestors, as it is today (NIV).

There is so much in this passage that I believe the Lord is speaking through today, and I will continue to unpack this and share as the Lord leads me to, but today I want to encourage you with this.

The Lord is bringing you into a good, new land. It is a land that is going to be a land of refreshing. There is going to be new wine, there is going to be healing, there is going to be increase, there is going to be abundant provision—the camels are coming. There is going to be financial increase for many of you. There is going to be favor, opportunity, increase, blessing upon blessing, hearts' desires fulfilled, tremendous fruitfulness, and your heart is going to *delight* and *be satisfied* in all that the Lord releases in you and to you. His heart is for you to *thrive* in your new land. There is going to be tremendous blessing.

Deuteronomy 1:11 says:

May the Lord, the God of your ancestors, increase you a thousand times and bless you as he has promised! (NIV)

There is going to be tremendous increase that you will receive, but in the midst of the increase, in the midst of the blessing I feel the heart of God so strongly: *"Don't forget Me."*

I feel a beautiful, loving warning from the heart of God that in the midst of the tremendous increase and blessing coming to you, stay deep in the secret place. Stay close to His heart, and I feel the Lord saying that as you stay deep in the secret place, *"You will remember."*

Be intentional to continue to *come away* with Him. He is bringing you in the midst of tremendous blessing and increase to a greater place of *union* with Him.

Obedience Over Opportunity

I have been talking a lot about this lately, but the Lord is having me repeat this over and over. *"Obedience over opportunity."* In this new land of blessing, of provision, of increase, stay close to His heart and seek His strategy. Seek His guidance and His *way* to steward all that He is releasing. For in this new land, there will be many opportunities, but the Lord is encouraging us to continue to choose Him and choose to obey His voice, no matter how sparkly the opportunity is that comes. Do not forget the commands of the Lord; do not forget the strategy that He has given you. Do not forget to hold to His decrees. For the "pathways" in this new land of significant increase may be completely different from what you expect and the Lord may have you "go against the grain," but I encourage you to *obey* His voice even when you don't understand.

I had a significant dream this year where the Lord showed me increase coming to the people of God and the wisdom that would be *needed* to steward the increase He is releasing. As I was waking, the Lord spoke to me: *"Lana, in this season, increase and wisdom are marrying."* So I implore you, in this season of incredible increase that is about to burst forth in a whole new way in the new lands, to be seeking the wisdom and strategy of God to know how to *steward* the land of incredible blessing and increase (see James 1:5).

Be Intentional to Remember: A Warning Against Pride

> *Otherwise, when you eat and are satisfied, when you build fine houses and settle down, and when your herds and flocks grow large and your silver and gold increase and all you have is multiplied, then your heart will become proud and you will forget the Lord your God, who brought you out of Egypt, out of the land of slavery* (Deuteronomy 8:12-14 NIV).

In this new land of increase and blessing, as we continue to remember His decrees and obey His voice, staying deep in the secret place, close to His heart, our hearts will be guarded. I felt the Lord saying, *"Be intentional to remember."* Be *intentional* to remember what He has done for you, who He is, and where you have "come from" in the place of incredible increase and blessing. Whatever that looks like for you, be purposeful to *remember* all He has done for you and brought you through.

Who brought you out of Egypt, out of the land of slavery.
He led you through the vast and dreadful wilderness, that
thirsty and waterless land, with its venomous snakes and
scorpions. He brought you water out of hard rock. He gave
you manna to eat in the wilderness, something your ances-
tors had never known, to humble and test you so that in
the end it might go well with you (Deuteronomy 8:14-16
NIV).

I felt this warning from the heart of such a beautiful
Father, our perfect heavenly Father, because He is wanting His people to be guarded from the place of pride. In
the new land of incredible blessing and increase, I saw
many beginning to struggle with pride, and pride creep-
ing into hearts, and a great "forgetting" was taking place,
but the Lord is releasing such a beautiful warning to us
as His people that as we enter into this place of incredible blessing and increase, that we stay deep in that place
of intimacy where He develops humility within us, He
refines by fire, He purifies, and He leads us. In this new
land as we live deep in the secret place, He is going to
bring about great rest, He is going to bring about great
refreshment, and He is going to continue to remove the
things within us that wage war against what He wants to
build and release.

So Much Is About to Change

So much is about to change! This is the season of radical
change, and I sense the strategy of the enemy to attempt
to lure hearts in their promised lands into a place of

busyness or hinder that quiet, secret place of deep place of intimacy with Jesus, because the enemy doesn't want us as God's people to know how to *steward* the increase; he wants it hindered.

But friend, I encourage you today—as the Lord leads you into this new land, as the blessing, the increase, the financial blessing, the breakthroughs explode all around you more and more—stay close to His heart. Be intentional to come away with Him and remember what He has done and from where you have come. There is a glorious new depth of intimacy awaiting you in your new land of promise. The Lord wants you to be filled with great joy, your heart glad and rejoicing in your blessing and the increase He is releasing upon you, but He also wants you to stay in the place of deep communion with Him. He wants to develop your union with Him in greater ways in the land of blessing.

The Lord whispered to me, "Many know how to steward the deep place of intimacy in hardship and trial and at times lack, but few know how to steward the deep place of intimacy in the increase, in the blessing, and in the abundant favor."

He wants to teach us in a whole new and fresh way how to steward increase and blessing with integrity, humility, and purity. I believe that is why it is so imperative, as He leads us into these new lands of increase and blessing, that we are sowing into the secret place of knowing Him and delighting in Him, our beautiful Jesus, as our true source, our first love, our all in all more than *ever* before.

I saw many of God's people swimming in the rivers of the Spirit at depths they had never experienced, moving in such a powerful flow of revelation of His Word and who He is as they stayed deep in the secret place. A whole new realm of flowing with Him, the leading of His Spirit, and being sensitive to heaven's strategy.

The land before you is *bountiful*, and in His heart and the secret place He will teach you to steward it and enjoy it with great joy!

Isn't the heart of God to encourage, to warn, and to prepare us stunning? He is so good. He is so loving and kind. God wants you and me to flourish in the new lands, and He wants us to run with Him in all that He has for us, so He is setting up divine parameters for that increase and acceleration that we are going to see.

Can we focus on Deuteronomy 8:11?

> *Be careful that you do not forget the Lord your God, failing to observe his commands, his laws and his decrees that I am giving you this day* (NIV).

As we enter into this new era when acceleration will be unprecedented; in the joy of it all; in the wonder of it all; in the amazing signs, wonders, and miracles we will see and what the hand of the Lord will do—I believe the Lord is setting us up to thrive in it all by releasing these warnings.

That is the heart of this chapter—that you would hear the voice of the Holy Spirit clearly, reminding you not to forget Him in all that you are going to see and all you are going to do in this new era with Him.

Don't Lose Me in the Breakthrough

I remember that day clearly when I heard the Lord say to me and to the body of Christ, *"Don't lose Me in the breakthrough, don't forget Me."* The love of God that I felt in that moment was indescribable. It wasn't a weak and needy God begging His people not to forget Him because He would feel rejected—of course not! It was the warning and release of wisdom from a loving Father, setting up those divine parameters for us to succeed in all He is releasing His people into.

See, it's easy in unprecedented acceleration to be drawn into a place of "it's all about me" and "what God is doing for me, in me, through me." The truth is, the more the acceleration is released, the greater opportunities and manifestations of His power and glory should lead us as His people *deeper* into that place of awe and wonder of who He is. This story isn't about us—it's about Jesus; it's about the Gospel being preached and what *He* did, not what *we* have done.

In this season of acceleration, I want to encourage you—if you are not falling more in love with Jesus and His Word, then take some time to withdraw and be with Him and allow Him to examine your heart and bring alignment, correction, healing, and reset.

There may be times when you feel things start to creep into your heart. Don't fall into condemnation, just run to Him. Keep short accounts with Him. The secret place is the place where you thrive. You and I live our lives in friendship with God and everything flows from that place.

So in Deuteronomy 8:11 the Lord releases the warning to not forget Him. Now let's look again at Deuteronomy 8:12-18:

> *Otherwise, when you eat and are satisfied, when you build*
> *fine houses and settle down, and when your herds and flocks*

131

grow large and your silver and gold increase and all you have is multiplied, then your heart will become proud and you will forget the Lord your God, who brought you out of Egypt, out of the land of slavery. He led you through the vast and dreadful wilderness, that thirsty and waterless land, with its venomous snakes and scorpions. He brought you water out of hard rock. He gave you manna to eat in the wilderness, something your ancestors had never known, to humble and test you so that in the end it might go well with you. You may say to yourself, "My power and the strength of my hands have produced this wealth for me." But remember the Lord your God, for it is he who gives you the ability to produce wealth, and so confirms his covenant, which he swore to your ancestors, as it is today (NIV).

So what is God saying here? "If you forget Me and forget what I have done, then pride creeps into your heart and you may say to yourself, 'My power and the strength of my hands have produced this wealth for me.'"

Let us never come to that place. I read that Scripture and meditate upon it and the fear of the Lord fills my heart. One of the biggest tests and temptations for believers in this era is going to be in the area of humility and the stewardship of the heart in the increase. I have talked about importance of humility in other chapters. As incredible as the acceleration and the demonstrated power of the Lord will be, it is also going to be a time of great purging and purifying. I heard the Lord whisper:

> **"This era of unprecedented acceleration is going to reveal the true motives and heart of My people."**

The Lord said that we have learned how to steward *lack* in past seasons and in many ways steward the contending process. Now as we move into rapid acceleration, we are going to have to learn as the body of Christ how to steward increase and this major move of His Spirit, and the alignment of the heart is key to this.

I remember the Lord saying to me recently:

> **"Hearts stay healthy in the secret place. Hearts stay healthy when they are close to My heart and in My Word."**

When I was sitting with the Lord preparing for this chapter, I felt strongly that the Lord wanted me to begin this chapter with this warning, because this warning brings us into the place of right alignment before Him to then move forward in stewarding the acceleration and the increase. So consider the first half of this chapter a loving foundational reminder from the Lord to take with you into this new era, as a major key to stewarding the acceleration that is going to take place.

It certainly is a time to get excited about what the Lord is doing. It is a time to really be expectant about the major move of His Spirit that is coming and the glorious preparation and purifying that's taking place now and will continue to bring us into right alignment with Him. It is all out of His love to bring us deeper into the glorious place of partnering with Him in all that He is going to do on the earth. Is there any greater privilege that has been given to us than being friends with God and making Him known in the earth? Even as I sit and write this now my heart fills with thankfulness and gratitude to Jesus for the gift of salvation so that I can be friends with God and then represent Him on the earth as His Spirit lives inside of me. I make it a priority to continue to take time in my week to sit with Him and just thank Him for that privilege.

Set Your Face as A Flint: Ferociously

Ferocious! This is the word that the Lord gave me in the beginning of 2019 to describe the level of faith that He was inviting us into. You will see this theme come up time and time again in this book because it's one of the main revelations the Lord has given me for this new era. The victorious bride is a ferocious bride—not ferocious in a negative, violent sense, but a passionate people who live in intentional faith with a roar of authority within them.

Ferocious means savagely fierce and extreme, and the ferocious bride stands in the authority given to her by Jesus (see Matt. 28:18-20; Eph. 2:6; Luke 10:19). I have to camp on Matthew 11:12 again here:

> *And from the time John the Baptist began preaching until now, the Kingdom of Heaven has been forcefully advancing, and violent people are attacking it* (NLT).

> *From the days of John the Baptist until now, the kingdom of heaven has been suffering violence, and the violent have been seizing it by force* (CSB).

> *From the moment John stepped onto the scene until now, the realm of heaven's kingdom is bursting forth, and passionate people have taken hold of its power* (TPT).

The picture there is clearly not one of inactivity. This is a picture of ferociousness; it's a picture of passionate people. Ever heard that saying "You're like a dog with a bone"? I had two puppies growing up, and the second one was a Jack Russell terrier named Beaut. Beaut was my best friend and I loved that dog so much. He had such a soft temperament, he was so faithful, he wouldn't leave my side, he was full of joy and bounced around everywhere. But let me tell you something—when Beaut was given a bone, he would guard that bone with every ounce of passion, strength, and drive within him. He turned into Beaut the Warrior! Once he had that bone, there was *no* way you were getting it off him. Beaut became ferocious. So are we to be with the promises of God in our lives, the Word of God in our lives, and advancing the Kingdom!

Guard Your Focus!

I am going to say that again, just in case you missed it—*guard your focus!*

In this new era of rapid acceleration, not only will there be a new realm of bold faith for us to walk in, there is and will be a battle over your *focus*. Deuteronomy 8 challenges our focus to remain on the Lord and not forget Him. Where do you place your *focus?*

I also believe that the Lord wants to encourage us to guard our hearts against *distraction* in this new era. I am sure we all know what distraction means, but me being the word nerd that I am, and the way God has given me such revelation through the meaning of words, I want to look at it here. *Collins English Dictionary* says, "A distraction is something that turns your attention away from something you want to concentrate on." Its synonyms are "disturbance, interference, diversion, interruption."

I want you to hear this. The Lord showed me a demonic spirit with a *specific assignment* to bring *distraction*. The Lord showed me that this demonic spirit is not only coming to distract God's people from intentional focus upon the Lord and what He is saying. It is coming to stop God's people from *advancing* the Kingdom of God through the assignment on their lives, *occupying* the land that God has for them, and *walking* in promises fulfilled.

This demonic spirit is coming intensely right now in 2020, but it will continue in this new era. It will attempt to cause God's people to become distracted with *everything else* rather than their time with the Lord, being in the Word, and the assignments of the Lord on their lives.

I want to pause here for a moment. This brings up a significant question, doesn't it? It brings up the question, what is the mandate on your life? Do you know it? Psalm 139:16 says that all our days are written in His book. We all have an assignment and plans/destiny for our lives. I was talking with a friend of mine recently, Adam F. Thompson, and we were talking about the blueprints and destiny that God has for each of our lives. Adam mentioned Jeremiah 6:16 to me, and since he brought this verse to my attention I have been meditating upon it. As Adam shared with me, it's the blueprint of God, the plans and destiny God has for us to walk in. I want to share that Scripture with you:

> *Stand at the crossroads and look; ask for the ancient paths, ask where the good way is, and walk in it, and you will find rest for your souls. But you said, "We will not walk in it"* (Jeremiah 6:16 NIV).

> *Thus says the Lord, "Stand by the roads and look; ask for the ancient paths, where the good way is; then walk in it, and you will find rest for your souls. But they said, 'We will not walk in it'"* (Jeremiah 6:16 AMP).

God has a plan and destiny for your life. There is a scroll in heaven with your name on it and the blueprint of God for your life. What He has called you to, specifically. If you don't know it, I encourage you to be asking the Lord for specific revelation on what is written on that scroll. I have had a few encounters with the Lord in the library of heaven, and Jesus has opened a book and I knew it was the book of my life. He began to show me glimpses of things He has planned for me and called me to (see Jer. 29:11), and when I see them then I agree with those blueprints and plans by faith and my obedience to walk out that call.

> *Then I said, "Behold, I have come to do your will, O God, as it is written of me in the scroll of the book"* (Hebrews 10:7 ESV).

Isaiah 50:7

So you and I in this new era of acceleration need to set out faces as flint and be *ferocious* against distraction (see Isa. 50:7). Whatever it is the Lord has called you to in this new era, go after it.

See, the Lord showed me that this demonic spirit bringing distraction is coming to hinder, and if it can convince you or I that it's just "natural" circumstances we are experiencing that are keeping us busy, we are going to fight it on a natural level. I am talking about relentless distraction, day after day. There just seems to be constant distraction from the things God has called you to do, your secret place with the Lord, and there's chaos surrounding it—that's not natural, that's spiritual. Recognize the pattern and go to war over it. Bind that spirit of distraction in the name of Jesus and be ferocious over guarding your time and your intentionality of *obedience*. The Lord showed me the enemy is going to use many things in an *accelerated way* in this era of divine acceleration to attempt to hinder God's people. He will use fears in the hearts of God's people, busyness, comparison, lies, discouragement, and many other things, even opportunities. Yes, I said opportunities. Some opportunities will come your way in this new era that are gloriously good, but that doesn't mean God is breathing on them. It's imperative to ask the Holy Spirit for discernment on which opportunities to walk in, because some will come to distract you from the God-breathed opportunity that will be before you. The key is to *recognize* hindrances and not bow to them.

Ask the Holy Spirit for guidance on how to stand against these distractions, because the enemy is trying to *steal* from you (see John 10:10). God is moving you into new realms of walking in abundant life and occupying, and that is why the battle is so fierce.

Stay in Your Lane

Do not get distracted in this new era by what others are doing. God showed me another strategy of the enemy is *comparison*. Do not look at what others are doing, their powerful giftings, or how fruitful their ministry is. Comparison will *steal* from you and cause you to withdraw.

I prophesy over you in this new era there is a greater awakening upon you of your identity in Christ. You are going to encounter the love of Jesus deeper than you ever have, breaking off and healing any insecurity that may try to steal from you and distract you in this new era. There is a thriving and blossoming the Lord wants to bring you into in this new era when you delight more than ever in His plans that He has for you and what He has written on the book of heaven for your life. Nestle deeply into His heart if you feel comparison coming to distract you and ask the Holy Spirit for His truth.

The anointing, the giftings, the calling, the blueprints that God has for your life are needed in the earth. Jesus in you and His light and love radiating through you in the giftings and mandate upon your life is *powerful* and won't look like the person next to you or your neighbor down the street. That's *good* and that's how God intended it. We are all a part of His glorious body (see 1 Cor. 12:12-27), and there is a greater "taking off" into His plans and destiny for your life in this new era that will take place through your obedience to Him and partnering with the Holy Spirit. Don't allow comparison to distract you.

Get Ferocious in Flint-Like Focus Using His Word

I cannot emphasize enough how important it is in this rapid acceleration when things are heating up and speeding up to be *grounded and founded in the Word.*

This demonic spirit bringing distraction has an agenda to keep you from the Word of God and to keep you in a place of confusion over what God is saying in this new era. I believe that the realm of revelation that has opened up to us, where the Lord is releasing His wisdom and insight to us, is deeper than we have ever walked in. Part of the distraction the enemy tries to bring is in the area of confusion and fogginess. The enemy wants to distract you with confusion, through other voices around you, and hinder your clarity and vision.

Again, tackle this not in the natural first. Take authority over this in the Spirit. Bind the spirit of confusion and witchcraft and mental fogginess (it's part of an attack of witchcraft) and begin to pray in the Spirit and decree the Word of God. When you feel the distraction coming on, go to war. Go to war with the Word. Search the Scriptures pertaining to the situation bringing distraction and war with the Word. Grab the prophetic words God has given you over the area where the distraction is attempting to steal, kill, and destroy and wage war with them (see 1 Tim. 1:8). Ask the Lord if there are any areas where this distraction has found legal ground, and allow the Holy Spirit to reveal any "landing pad." It could be an agreement with a lie; it could be fear. If there's anything in the heart that the enemy is using to keep you distracted, ask the Holy Spirit and He will show you. Repent of the landing pad and invite the Lord to speak His truth. Place the Word of God over those areas through your faith and move forward in flint-like focus on what He has said and see the distraction flee.

It's time to get ferociously focused on knowing Jesus and on what He is saying and what He is calling you to do in this new era. This is your time to take ground, to occupy, to see the hand of the Lord bring acceleration and do things you've never dreamed. Don't allow *anything* to steal your focus and distract you. Get ferocious with distraction. That doesn't mean being rude, unkind, or angry with people; it means being passionately dedicated in this era of acceleration, making the decision on what your priorities are, and obeying the Lord and giving 100 percent to all He is putting before you. This is the preparation to walk in that and agree with the divine parameters the Lord sets.

My heart is that the keys He has released in and through this chapter are like a lighthouse shining its light for you in these new, uncharted territories to lead you into new waters and keep you from crashing upon any rocks. This is the era for you to take your place and run with Him into the most glorious adventure of seeing His glory manifest upon the earth. What will take place in a day will be unprecedented, leaving you in awe and wonder of One alone—*Jesus Christ!*

Chapter Eight

STEWARDSHIP

*O*ver the past five years, the Lord has been speaking to me so much about stewardship. Our stewardship of what the Lord has placed in our hands is of the utmost importance. The Lord cares about how we steward that which He has placed in our hands.

Look at the parable of the talents in Matthew 25:14-30. As I meditate on this passage of Scripture, I read every line, every verse slowly. I am overcome by the weight of stewardship that we are called to as the body of Christ. Can we take a moment together and read this story?

Again, the Kingdom of Heaven can be illustrated by the story of a man going on a long trip. He called together his servants and entrusted his money to them while he was gone. He gave five bags of silver to one, two bags of silver to another, and one bag of silver to the last—dividing it in proportion to their abilities. He then left on his trip.

The servant who received the five bags of silver began to invest the money and earned five more. The servant with two bags of silver also went to work and earned two more. But the servant who received the one bag of silver dug a hole in the ground and hid the master's money.

After a long time their master returned from his trip and called them to give an account of how they had used his money. The servant to whom he had entrusted the five bags of silver came forward with five more and said, "Master, you gave me five bags of silver to invest, and I have earned five more."

The master was full of praise. "Well done, my good and faithful servant. You have been faithful in handling this small amount, so now I will give you many more responsibilities. Let's celebrate together!"

The servant who had received the two bags of silver came forward and said, "Master, you gave me two bags of silver to invest, and I have earned two more."

The master said, "Well done, my good and faithful servant. You have been faithful in handling this small amount, so now I will give you many more responsibilities. Let's celebrate together!"

Then the servant with the one bag of silver came and said, "Master, I knew you were a harsh man, harvesting crops you didn't plant and gathering crops you didn't cultivate. I was afraid I would lose your money, so I hid it in the earth. Look, here is your money back."

But the master replied, "You wicked and lazy servant! If you knew I harvested crops I didn't plant and gathered crops I didn't cultivate, why didn't you deposit my money in the bank? At least I could have gotten some interest on it."

Then he ordered, "Take the money from this servant, and give it to the one with the ten bags of silver. To those who use well what they are given, even more will be given, and they will have an abundance. But from those who do nothing, even what little they have will be taken away. Now throw this useless servant into outer darkness, where there will be weeping and gnashing of teeth" (NLT).

From this passage, as I read these words and truly let them sink in, I feel the weight of responsibility in stewarding that which God has placed in our hands. It is not about getting everything "right" and doing things "perfectly." I believe it is about the heart and it is about being faithful in obedience to the Lord and what He asks of us.

I often think about the responsibility that has been given to us as believers. We haven't been given a "brand name" to represent or a "large company" to represent; this is the King of kings and the Lord of lords who has given us a mandate and commission upon the earth.

And Jesus came and said to them, "All authority in heaven and on earth has been given to me. Go therefore and make disciples of all nations, baptizing them in the name of the

Father and of the Son and of the Holy Spirit, teaching them to observe all that I have commanded you. And behold, I am with you always, to the end of the age" (Matthew 28:18-20 ESV).

We have been given the greatest privilege we will ever be given on earth. To know Jesus and be invited into relationship with Him and make Him known on the earth.

I have sought the Lord's heart for a long time, asking the Holy Spirit to develop in me a heart that stewards well. That stewards with purity and integrity that which He places in my hand and entrusts to me. Why? Because I love Him. Out of our love for Jesus and living in deep communion with Him, our hearts flourish in the place of worship before Him. We desire to steward well all that He has placed in our hands. It is *from* the place of intimacy where the heart of healthy stewardship flourishes.

In this last year, I have been feeling the Holy Spirit bringing me back to the basics. He is showing me the powerful truth in the simplicity. The simple yet life-changing truths, the simple yet powerful foundation, that the more I know Him, the more I am going to look like Him.

The more time I spend with Him, the more I am going to know His ways, His heart, His voice, and reflect Him in the earth. I have had so many moments when I have been sitting with Him and just enjoying Him and hearing His heart. I watch as His love pours over me, as His voice comforts me and strengthens me; simply being with Him brings me to life. I sit there and I hear a voice that calls me higher. I hear a voice that calls out who I really am and separates the lies from the truth, the light from the darkness. I sit with Him and He unravels His heart, His plans, and His dreams for my life. I find myself sitting with Him and my heart is unraveled and I am left breathless by His goodness. The more I see Him, the more I love Him. The more I see Him, the more I want Him. The more I see Him, the more I trust Him. The more I see Him, the more I abandon myself to Him and His ways. I think of my history with Him, I think of the glorious mountaintop places, and I think of the deepest, darkest valleys, and in every place I see His goodness; I see His love.

I close my eyes and I think of my beautiful Jesus on the Cross. I think of every lash He took for me; I think of every moment of pain and heartache He endured for me, taking on all of my sin—and not just all of my sin, but the sin of the world. The entire world. While I was yet a sinner, He died for me (see Rom. 5:8). He didn't hold anything back; He gave it all for me. Everything, because that's how much He loves and values me. John 3:16 isn't just a lovely verse that we put on bumper stickers and bookmarks; it's a life-changing, transforming verse:

> *For God so loved the world, that he gave his only Son, that whoever believes in him should not perish but have eternal life* (ESV).

> *For this is how much God loved the world—he gave his one and only, unique Son as a gift. So now everyone who believes in him will never perish but experience everlasting life* (TPT).

I love what Brian Simmons wrote in *The Passion Translation*'s commentary notes on John 3:16: "Or 'God proved he loved the world by giving his Son.'"

Think about that for a second. He proved He loved the world by giving His Son so that we may experience everlasting life when we believe in Him. The revelation of John 3:16 is going to explode in this new era. The Lord is going to further awaken the body of Christ to the revelation of His *proven, displayed* love that is going to break the lies and chains that have haunted and tormented many for decades. There is a fire of the love of God through John 3:16 that is going to set hearts alight in the earth like never before.

Do you know what shocked me? The Lord showed me that indeed John 3:16 is going to explode in the earth and God is going to draw those who do not yet know Jesus to Him through the demonstration of His love. But the Lord also showed me that there is a revival of the love of God coming upon the Church to reignite hearts again. The Lord showed me that there are many in the body of Christ who need a revival of John 3:16 for their own lives and for the passion of sharing the good news of the Gospel to explode within their hearts. There is already a mighty awakening taking place in the body of Christ, and we are beginning to see the Church rise up and begin to declare the good news of the Gospel and the wave of evangelism begin to explode. The Lord spoke to me that this is just the tip of the iceberg; these are just the first few trickles of what we are going to see as far as an awakening of John 3:16 in the Church. The greater awakening that is going to take place will summon the people of God into a greater level of stewardship.

In the place of deep intimacy with Him, sitting close to His heart, sitting in His Word, I cannot help but be changed. I am changed. I cannot remain the same. I cannot see Him and remain as I am. I change when I see Him. I step more into life. I step more into who I am. I step further into truth. I step into strength. I step into peace. I step into awakening. So as I cultivate my life being a friend of God, part of the fruit of my friendship with God is my stewardship of all that He has given me. As I live in the place of love, loving Jesus, I cannot help but want to pour out my life and give Him my best. I don't want to give Him the scraps. I don't want to give Him the leftovers; I want to give Him the best.

I remember in 2011 I landed in Chico, California on a word of the Lord to join Youth with a Mission. I remember the excitement, anticipation, and fear of stepping into this new adventure with Jesus on the other side of the planet. I remember the hunger that I felt—such desperation in me to know Jesus and to encounter His heart deeper than I ever had before. In the first few weeks of our discipleship training school, they began to teach on worship, and my life was changed. Why? Because for the first time in my life I was introduced to the revelatory truth that worship isn't just singing to the Lord, *worship is a lifestyle.* Everything I do is worship to the Lord.

> *Therefore, whether you eat or drink, or whatever you do, do all to the glory of God* (1 Corinthians 10:31).

What a life-changing revelation that was for me as a young girl in her 20s. It opened up a whole new world for me that I was called to steward every area of my life well as my worship to Him. Why? *Because I love Him.*

I do not attempt to cultivate a heart or life of stewardship because I am scared He is going to yell at me or I am going to be in big trouble. That is not the stewardship of a son/daughter of God; that's the stewardship of an orphan. I attempt to steward my heart and live well because I love Him. Out of a healthy fear of God and who He is, I want to honor Him and worship Him with everything that I have. I shared on the fear of the Lord in Chapter Five, but I want to touch on it again for a moment here. I love what John Bevere says:

> The fear of the Lord is our only protection from hypocrisy.
>
> So many Christians have an unhealthy fear of God. They see Him as an angry tyrant waiting to drop the hammer when they mess up. If you think about God this way, you'll have a very hard time wanting to be around Him. A healthy fear of God is to have a proper reverence and awe for who He is. It causes us to want to draw near, not shrink back.
>
> The fear of God isn't to be scared of Him. It's to be terrified of being away from Him.[1]

As I have shared previously, a mighty move of His Spirit is going to take place to restore the fear of the Lord. The Church is going to tremble again as the holiness and the majesty of God are displayed. The restoration of the fear of God is going to bring forth a huge purging in the Church unlike anything we have ever seen and cause the body of Christ to awaken and walk in holiness and reverential fear of God that is going to shape and change the world in unprecedented ways. I am so thankful for John Bevere and others and how they have forerun with this message on the fear of God as it is about to manifest in monumental ways in this new era. Some of the most powerful gatherings and times of encountering the Lord will be when He shows up in His weighty presence so strongly that there is divine silence or, as Kathryn Kuhlman called it, "a holy hush." In those silent moments when you can't move because His glory is so thick and heavy, monumental things will take place in the lives of believers by the Spirit of God.

Part of the fear of the Lord that is beginning to weigh heavily is in this area of stewardship and stewarding with purity, integrity, and humility. Yes, we are called to steward our giftings, our ministry, our families, our homes, our marriages, our workplaces, but does that mean getting everything right? Does stewardship mean doing everything perfectly? No, it doesn't. The Lord showed me that faithful stewardship is about the heart. It begins in the heart.

The Stewardship of the Heart

In this new era there is going to be a greater uncovering of impurity, because the Lord is preparing the Church. He is coming back for a pure and spotless bride (see Eph. 5:26-27), cleansed by the washing with water through the Word (we will come back to this point in a moment). Part of the refining that must take place in this new era is the refining and purifying of the heart. The Lord has already begun in many ways to purge and purify hearts, and this has been happening in the place of contending, in the place of battle, in the place of many valleys. Now, I am not saying that there will not be battles or giants and valleys in this new era. There will be, but one of the greatest tests of this new era will be the *stewardship of increase and acceleration.*

In this next great move of the Spirit of God, the Lord is speaking about His glory that is going to be demonstrated in unprecedented ways, miraculous ways. There is going to be a testing of the heart that is going to take place. The testing will be in how we steward the greatest move of God that we have ever seen. It is the testing of the heart in new levels of favor, in the hand of God repositioning, in the direction He leads, in the way He moves, in the increase, in the supernatural and miraculous that will be demonstrated.

The Lord spoke to me that one of the greatest tests of the heart in this new era will be the place of keeping it all about Jesus and not touching His glory. When the Lord spoke this to me it shook me to the core. It

149

shook me in a healthy place of the fear of God to fall on my face before Him and cry out to Him like David in Psalm 139:23-24:

> *Search me, O God, and know my heart! Try me and know my thoughts! And see if there be any grievous way in me, and lead me in the way of everlasting!* (ESV)

> *God, I invite your searching gaze into my heart. Examine me through and through; find out everything that may be hidden within me. Put me to the test and sift through all my anxious cares. See if there is any path of pain I'm walking on, and lead me back to your glorious, everlasting ways— the path that brings me back to you* (TPT).

In August 2019, I had an encounter with the Lord and I heard the Lord say, *"There is an intense firing of My hand upon the hearts of many leaders and fivefold ministers right now."* The Lord was calling them to yield to it and embrace it, for He was preparing them to partner with Him to see the greatest move of His Spirit that they had ever seen.

In this encounter the Lord showed me what was taking place. The firing had increased significantly, and the Lord was deeply purging. The Lord went on to speak to me about this being a time of deep consecration.

> *Then Joshua said to the people, "Consecrate yourselves, for tomorrow the Lord will do wonders among you"* (Joshua 3:5 ESV).

The Lord was speaking about removing impurities, purging mixture, dealing with complacency and compromise, and the fire of His love to see God's people and especially leadership walk in holiness. It isn't something found in a place of striving to be holy but in a place of deep intimacy with the King.

The Lord continued to speak to me about things changing rapidly in the body of Christ. We are in a time when things are not remaining as they were. We have entered a new era and God is doing a new thing (see Isa. 43:19). It requires a laid-down leadership and fivefold ministry that is completely surrendered to His way and His process. I felt the urgency of the hour upon leadership and fivefold ministers to "do business" with the Holy Spirit and allow the firing of His hand upon them to remove together any troubling foxes that come to spoil the vine (see Song of Songs 2:15). In this encounter, the love of God was so strong. His heart resounded loudly that the firing was not for harm but for their good. It's part of the preparation to walk in more.

I was shaken in this encounter when I heard the Holy Spirit say, *"In this new era I am removing many leaders and fivefold ministers from thrones they have placed themselves on and I am taking My rightful place."*

The Lord spoke this specifically for the prophetic word He had me release in August, and from then on He has continued to speak to me about the mighty shift that will take place where He will be removing many leaders and fivefold ministers from thrones they have placed themselves on. What does that speak of? It speaks of pride. It speaks of alignment. It speaks of the Lord taking His rightful place as King of kings and Lord of lords and the One who receives the glory.

You may recognize how these themes are flowing throughout the chapters. That's because these are some of the biggest issues holding the Church back. This firing of the Lord in this new era is not condemnation, for the Lord does not condemn. In Christ we are righteous; in Christ we are pure, we are forgiven, we are cleansed by the blood of the Lamb (see 1 John 1:7). The Lord is not speaking about identity; He is speaking about stewardship.

As I have continued to seek His heart the same warning that was upon the leadership and fivefold ministers is upon the body of Christ. There is a high call to consecration in the stewardship of what the Lord will do in this new era. There is a call to "come out" of impurity and areas of compromise and walk in abandonment to the Lord.

The call to intimacy is getting louder in this new era. In order to steward the heart well, we must be people living close to His heart and in *surrender. A key to stewardship in this new era is surrender.* It is that place of surrender that invites the Holy Spirit to come and have His way, the place of yielding that gives Him access.

Fresh Surrender

> *I appeal to you therefore, brothers, by the mercies of God, to present your bodies as a living sacrifice, holy and acceptable to God, which is your spiritual worship. Do not be conformed to this world, but be transformed by the renewal of your mind, that by testing you may discern what is the will of God, what is good and acceptable and perfect* (Romans 12:1-2 ESV).

> *Beloved friends, what should be our proper response to God's marvelous mercies? I encourage you to surrender yourselves to God to be his sacred, living sacrifices. And live in holiness, experiencing all that delights his heart. For this becomes your genuine expression of worship* (Romans 12:1 TPT).

It's the place of encounter with Jesus where you sit with Him and lay it all on the table again and allow Him to rearrange and change whatever needs to be rearranged and changed. It's the place of encounter with the Lord where you and I sit with Him and invite Him to examine our hearts and cry out for His fire and embrace it when it comes.

I love the first line of that song: "If the altar's where You meet us, take me there, take me there." Make it a daily place of positioning to live on the altar. We are in an era when the Lord is calling His people back upon the altar so that His fire can fall. We should never get off the altar—the place of being living sacrifices. The whole idea and picture of a living sacrifice speaks of surrender.

It's not the place of "fighting on the altar." It's the place where it is a *joy* to surrender and be that living sacrifice. Why? Because you love Him! Because I love Him! Because we live not for our own names to be exalted but live for His name to be lifted high and His name glorified. For Jesus to receive His *full* reward.

He is going to set your heart on fire in this new era, burning with a love for Him like never before as you position yourself before Him and seek His heart with humility. He is going to set your heart burning for Him and His ways, bringing forth the greatest alignment in your life that you have ever experienced.

The reason the Lord is repeating over and over again to take stewardship in this new era very seriously is because He wants you to walk in *all* that He has for you. He doesn't want you to miss a thing. He wants you to walk closely with Him and in all that He has planned for your life and what is written in your book in heaven by the hand of God (see Jer. 29:11). Because of the magnitude of what He is releasing in this new era, there is a greater consecration that the Lord is requiring. There is a level of purity, humility, and integrity that has always been the call for the Church to walk in, but she has swayed away from it.

This is the era when the Lord is bringing the Church back to the first love. The purging isn't comfortable at times—it's painful. The dealings of the Lord don't always leave you with Holy Ghost goose bumps, but the dealing of the Lord is *always* for your good, because He is a good Father. I spoke in Chapter Six about the correction of the Lord that is going to be experienced in this new era. The Church is going to learn in greater ways the correction of the Lord in His love as a good Father who is bringing His people to further maturity.

The Lord spoke to me recently that it is time for the Church to *grow up!* Part of that growing up and maturing is going to be found in the intensifying of the purifying fire that is going to be revealed in this new era that will usher His people who embrace it into new realms of walking in the supernatural and carrying the genuine move of His Spirit in the earth.

Ask for Specific Strategies of Stewardship

One thing we must always remember is this: God is more willing to answer, pour out, and teach us than we are willing to receive sometimes. In our position of "asking," He will not turn us away. In the area of stewardship, I heard the Holy Spirit say, *"Ask for specific strategies of stewardship."*

God is releasing blueprint strategies, downloads, and revelations to navigate this new era on unprecedented levels. He wants to give you specific strategies to steward your heart, your finances, your family, your children, your ministry, the favor He releases on your life, your job. He doesn't sit on the sidelines and say, "Make sure you steward well," and then leave you to work it out. He is the God who wants to teach you. The Holy Spirit is your helper, He is going to lead you into all truth, and He is the God of wisdom (see John 14:26; 16:13;

James 1:5). God has *specific* strategies for you in the stewardship of all that He has for you. Ask Him! Then obey what He tells you and you will find greater life and increase. As Joseph received a specific download of wisdom from God in the interpretation of Pharaoh's dream (see Gen. 41), he was then put in charge of all of Egypt. There are specific strategies that God wants to give you to help you steward what He is releasing—the increase and the move of God in this new era— that will be astonishing, and part of that stewardship is receiving His wisdom and knowing His heart and His ways.

I Heard the Lord Say, "Don't Waste Water"

In this new era when the Lord is highlighting stewardship so strongly, the Lord spoke to me very clearly about the stewardship of the revelation that He is releasing. As I was in my prayer room, He spoke these words over the Church: *"Don't waste water."*

As I continued to seek His heart on this, the Lord showed me a tidal wave of revelation of His heart and His Word that is building and increasing right now in the body of Christ and will continue to in this new era. There is a portal of revelation that has opened up, releasing the strategies and wisdom of God in this new era that is unlike anything we have ever seen. When He spoke those words—*"Don't waste water"*—the fear of God came over me. The Lord was speaking about the "stewarding" of His voice and the revelation of His Word. The Lord is asking His people in this new era to ask for wisdom (see James 1:5), and that must be one of our greatest prayers. He is asking His people to walk in greater *wisdom* in stewarding the revelation that He is releasing.

So I asked the Lord for practical ways to steward His revelation. Every word that He speaks, I want to catch it. I don't want to miss a moment; I don't want to miss a word. I want to live so close to Him that not only can I hear His voice but I hear the *tone* in which He speaks it. In order for me to hear His tone, I have to know His nature. I am going to mention lingering here again, because I want you to look at a Scripture with me, and it is key in stewardship.

1. Marinate and Linger

For the past few years, the Lord has been speaking to me about lingering. I love Exodus 33:11:

> *Thus the Lord used to speak to Moses face to face, as a man speaks to his friend. When Moses turned again into the camp, his assistant Joshua the son of Nun, a young man, would not depart from the tent* (ESV).

I had a powerful dream many years ago and the Lord spoke to me: *"Lana, I am looking for those who will linger. For to those who will linger, I will entrust the secrets of My heart."*

We must be people who do not rush out of His presence. We must be people who are sitting with Him to linger with Him to hear His heart because we want to know Him deeply. The Lord spoke to me recently and His words stunned me:

"I am bringing great alignment in the Church in this new era, where the worship of revelation will be brought down through repentance, and a purity of knowing Me and worshiping Me in spirit and in truth will arise. My Spirit will bring conviction upon many where there has been a worship of revelation and who has the greater revelation, rather than the joy and purity in friendship with Me and seeking to know Me because of love for Me."

Numerous times over the past few years the Lord has spoken something to me that continues to leave me in a place of the fear of the Lord in the stewardship of His voice. I heard Him speaking over the body of Christ: *"Do not prostitute My voice."* Wow! He began to show me in many different ways the impurity and "misuse" of His voice and the revelation He releases. The Lord will deal with the impurity in hearts that would use His voice or revelation to build their platforms or manipulate for their own personal gain. God is dealing with spiritual prostitution and impurity in many areas, especially in the area of the stewardship of His voice and revelation. I will share more about this in Chapter Twelve. Where the voice of the Lord has been used to build platforms for people and self-promotion, the fire of God is coming down upon those areas to convict and correct. It is His goodness to bring forth repentance and lead people into deeper encounter with Him and purity in the stewardship of the revelation and the word He is releasing.

Again, these words of the Lord highlight areas of the heart. If our pursuit is of revelation and who has the "latest" and "best" revelation or prophetic word, then there are issues of the heart the Lord wants to purify and realign.

As He spoke, *"Marinate and linger,"* I had a vision of Jesus, and He was inviting His people into *deep waters* of revelation. They began to enter the waters with their feet, and as they would hear the voice of God and the revelation He was releasing from His Word they would run on that revelation. Jesus was standing in the middle of this ocean of revelation, and there were depths to be explored and received. The Lord continued to speak over and over, *"This is the era of Daniel 2:22 and Jeremiah 33:3."*

He reveals deep and hidden things; he knows what is in the darkness, and the light dwells with him (Daniel 2:22 ESV).

Call to Me and I will answer you, and will tell you great and hidden things that you have not known (Jeremiah 33:3 ESV).

There is a *depth* of revelation of the Word of God and His heart that He wants to release. Do not be quick to run on the revelation He is releasing. Marinate and linger, for if you run too quickly out of the water you will not receive the depth of revelation the Lord has for you. There is an unprecedented level of revelation that the Lord has for *His friends* and those who will linger.

There's a private place reserved for the lovers of God, where they sit near him and receive the revelation-secrets of his promises (Psalm 25:14 TPT).

2. Be Discerning Who You Share With

"Don't waste what is holy on people who are unholy. Don't throw your pearls to pigs! They will trample the pearls, then turn and attack you" (Matt. 7:6 NLT). What God is speaking and releasing right now and what He is going to continue to release into this new era is His desire to teach the people of God greater wisdom in the delivery and sharing of the revelation. *Not everything the Lord shares with you is to be shared publicly, and not everything He speaks is to be shared with everyone.* When the Lord spoke to me: *"It's time for the Church to grow up!"* the sense also surrounded me that it is time for the people of God to walk in the meat of the Word of God. To walk in maturity in the depth of revelation He is releasing and then *how* it is released. I kept hearing Hebrews 5:12-14:

*For though by this time you ought to be teachers, you need
someone to teach you again the basic principles of the oracles
of God. You need milk, not solid food, for everyone who lives
on milk is unskilled in the word of righteousness, since he is
a child. But solid food is for the mature, for those who have
their powers of discernment trained by constant practice to
distinguish good from evil* (Hebrews 5:12-14 ESV).

In this new era, it will be clear who has had their powers of discernment trained by constant practice in the distinguishing of good
from evil and who knows the deep revelation of the word of righteousness. There is also an invitation from the Lord to not remain on milk
but to partner with Him in the process of the maturing that He is
doing in the Church. In relation to the wisdom of the Lord to not
share everything He speaks, the Lord released a warning to me for us
as God's people out of Genesis 37, when Joseph ran in excitement, passion, and immaturity and shared the revelation of his future that the
Lord had showed him through dreams. The Lord is calling the people
of God to be wise and let His Spirit lead them to share the revelation
He is releasing. It is not only for their protection but also part of the
process of maturely stewarding the revelation and secrets of His heart
that He releases.

3. Write It Down

The Lord spoke to me very clearly that we must take account of
what He speaks. Be specific in writing down all that He is speaking.
Write down dates; write down times. The sense was so strong around
me as He spoke, *"Keep a record."* If you don't journal or find it hard to
write it all down, record it on your phone. Find a way to keep a record.
If you steward His voice well and place value on it by recording it, writing it down, meditating on it, etc., He will not only give you more, but

you will begin to see greater clarity of what He is speaking as you see it all piecing together. The year 2020 and beyond is the era when we will *see* like we have never seen before, and part of that *seeing more* is to steward well what *He sees* and what *He* speaks. Keep account!

Let us be people who continue to ask the Holy Spirit for wisdom and give Him permission to teach us, correct us, purify, purge, align, and position us in the stewardship of all He releases for His glory (see James 1:5). May our stewardship of every area of our lives be worship to and bring glory to Him.

Note

1. John Bevere, "Reset 2020 Day Three: FEAR!" Facebook.com, January 3, 2020, https://www.facebook.com/JohnBevere.page.

Chapter Nine

THE FEROCIOUS FOCUS OF FAITH AND A NEW LEVEL OF NORMAL

The call to "come up higher" is resounding in the body of Christ in this new era. What do I mean by that? It's the call to victorious living. The Lord has spoken to me over and over again that He isn't raising up chickens; He is raising up eagles.

I had a vision in which I saw many in the body of Christ running around on the ground like chickens. When I saw this vision, there was a very strong sense of "living on the ground," and the phrase kept coming to me that I would often hear as a child in the school playground: "You're a chicken," speaking of someone who is in fear and too scared to do something. There was a move of the Spirit and invitation to partner with the Lord to walk in a bold faith that has not been walked in before. The transition from the chicken to the eagle. The place of victorious living by faith.

In this new era, the Holy Spirit is maturing the saints in the Word of God and the decree of the Word. The Lord is bringing us further into our seat. Ephesians 2:6 says:

> *For he raised us from the dead along with Christ and seated us with him in the heavenly realms because we are united with Christ Jesus* (NLT).

> *He raised us up with Christ the exalted One, and we ascended with him into the glorious perfection and authority of the heavenly realm, for we are now co-seated as one with Christ!* (TPT)

He is bringing us as His people further into the victory that is ours in Christ. He is teaching us as believers in this new era what it means to live by faith—to walk by faith and not by sight (see 2 Cor. 5:7).

This invitation upon us right now is to *decide* and take our stand upon the Word of God like never before. This era of unprecedented displays of His power and miracles is going to come through a people who live, breathe, feast, and walk upon the Word of God and live from that place. Hebrews 11:3 says:

> *By faith [that is, with an inherent trust and enduring confidence in the power, wisdom and goodness of God] we understand that the worlds (universe, ages) were framed and created [formed, put in order, and equipped for their*

intended purpose] by the word of God, so that what is seen was not made out of things which are visible (AMP).

So by the power of the Word of God and by faith, we root and anchor our expectancy.

A New Level of Normal: The Ferocious Focus of Faith

In the middle of 2018, I had an encounter with the Lord where He was continually speaking to me about the increase of faith that was coming upon the body of Christ. The Lord showed me the pressures, the battles, the fires many have faced and are facing, but in the midst of the pressure, the pressing, and the opposition, the Spirit of God is raising up the people of God to a new level of faith.

That's when the Holy Spirit whispered these words to me: *"Lana, I am now raising My people up to a new level of normal."*

I had a vision in which I saw many of God's people being pushed into a corner, battle weary and feeling the intensity of the pressure, when suddenly Jesus appeared in front of them. He placed His hand on their chests, and in the middle of the pressing and pressure, with such a weariness and panic on many faces, He spoke so gently but full of authority: *"Look at Me! Look at Me!"*

It was an invitation to look at *nothing else* but Him. He then spoke again, and these words penetrated every part of me: *"It's time for the ferocious focus of faith."*

As we saw in Chapter Seven, *ferocious* means savagely fierce, violent, intense, strong, powerful, and extreme. In the natural, *ferocious* often has negative connotations, but when the Lord spoke it my spirit leapt. It was the invitation to aggressively, violently, passionately come against every situation, every opposition, every giant with a violent conviction of faith that says, "My God said it, He promised it, His Word is true, I am not moving from it!" Matthew 11:12 is such a powerful verse for us here:

> From the moment John stepped onto the scene until now, the realm of heaven's kingdom is bursting forth, and passionate people have taken hold of its power (TPT).

> From the days of John the Baptist until now the kingdom of heaven suffers violent assault, and violent men seize it by force [as a precious prize] (AMP).

The vision continued. As the hand of Jesus was placed upon the chests of His people, I knew there was a major increase and impartation of faith taking place. Eye to eye in intense focus, gazes locked together, He spoke: *"It is now time to roar."*

Suddenly, I saw this fire burn within God's people—a fire of conviction of the *truth* and *power* of His Word and a righteous anger at what the enemy has stolen. The roar that burst forth out of the mouths of God's people was the Word of God, and it came with a boldness and conviction of faith greater than they had carried before.

> So shall my word be that goes out from my mouth; it shall not return to me empty, but it shall accomplish that which I purpose, and shall succeed in the thing for which I sent it (Isaiah 55:11 ESV).

> Is not my word like fire, declares the Lord, and like a hammer that breaks the rock in pieces? (Jeremiah 23:29 ESV)

In this vision, I saw Jesus turn to me and He said, *"Lana, pay attention to the roar. Listen to the roar. Listen to the sound of doubt being removed."*

I leaned in and listened to the roar of the conviction of truth and power of the Word flowing from the mouths of God's people, but something deep was taking place in their hearts. It was such a deep awakening to who He was—that Jesus *is* the Word (see John 1:1)—and areas of unbelief were being exposed in their hearts. I started hearing a sound. It was a *loud* sound, and it was the sound of *repentance.*

The sound of repentance was loudly bursting from within hearts and out of mouths. Repentance for aligning with doubt and allowing "natural realities" and "disappointments" to fester doubt in their hearts (I am going to talk more about this as we go on in this chapter). God was bringing deep healing, deliverance, and freedom in repentance, and He was increasing faith and the revelation of who He is and the power of His Word so significantly that doubt was being removed and a people were arising *strong* and *fortified.*

Now I want to stop here for a second. We are going to see a mighty wave of the Holy Spirit crash into the Church in this new era that is going to bring forth a major move of repentance. In September 2019, I had an encounter with the Lord and He said to me, *"Lana, a wave of travail is about to crash into the Church in this new era."* The Lord showed me that this wave of travail is coming with the restoration of the fear of the Lord to the Church. There it is again—the fear of the Lord! I heard the Lord say, *"My people are going to weep over sin again, ushering in the greatest move of holiness that we have ever seen."*

When the Lord spoke this, the sense surrounded me so strongly that this *weeping* over sin was not a place of condemnation, nor was it a place of not living in the revelation of our identity in Christ and our righteousness before Him (see 2 Cor. 5:21; Rom. 3:22). It was the place of the birthing of no toleration of sin; it was the place of consecration; it was the place of purity being birthed in the Church *because* of our love, awe, and wonder of who He is as the King of kings and Lord of lords. This deep repentance is going to take place in different ways in the Church in this new era to prepare us to carry the fire of His presence in ways we have never seen and be able to carry the influx of the mighty harvest of souls that will come into the Kingdom along with mighty signs, wonders, and miracles.

Now, why am I sharing this with you here? Because in this encounter, the Lord exposed the areas of unbelief in the hearts of His people. Jesus refers to unbelief many times in Scripture and how it can hinder faith and the miraculous (see Matt. 8:26; 13:54-58; 17:20). The "new normal" of faith that God will raise the Church up into in this new era is going to expose unbelief in significant ways. In one of the encounters I had with the Lord, I heard the Gospel being preached, but it shocked me when I saw *where* it was being preached—it was being preached *to the Church!*

Now, I have shared with you in previous chapters about how the Lord is going to awaken the Church in greater ways than we have ever seen to the *power* of the finished work of the Cross and the Gospel of His resurrection. He is going to deal mightily with unbelief in hearts. The revelation of Jesus and His love at Calvary will pour into hearts in this new era. This increasing awakening is going to bring forth a greater level of repentance for areas of the heart full of unbelief, which will lead His people into a greater realm of victory that is already theirs in Christ (see Rom. 8:37). Kenneth Copeland says:

> Unbelief is believing something other than what God has said about a situation. You can believe Jesus was raised

from the dead, you can believe He is your Lord, you can believe He is coming soon, but if you don't believe and do what He says, you are operating in unbelief. You can believe in Him, but still not believe what He says. The Bible calls this an evil heart—a hardened heart (Hebrews 3:12). And a heart of unbelief grieves God.[1]

The Lord is going to expose those areas of unbelief in the heart. Why? So we can move into a new level of normal and walk in the miraculous.

No Toleration

In this encounter with the Lord, as the Spirit of God was dealing with unbelief and God's people were partnering with the conviction of His Spirit, I saw the *intolerance* within them increase. That intolerance was for things in the natural that don't align with what God says, His purposes, plans, and Kingdom. As the intolerance rose and faith rose, the giants standing in opposition to the Word of God began losing their hold as the people of God were arising with a fire in their belly that said, "*No more!* I do not have to accept that for my life, my family, my city, my nation, the world. *Not on my watch!*"

There was a greater awakening taking place to the "standard and the normal," and that standard and normal was *the Word*. Where God's people had become chickens running on the ground and had lowered their expectations and lowered their theology to meet their experience, God was now calling them higher—to stand on the Word of God alone and what He speaks (see Matt. 4:4).

I remember the day a few years ago when God challenged me personally about this. One of my sons was sick, and I messaged a friend and asked her to pray for him. She replied lovingly, "Of course I will pray for him, but remember, Lana, it is normal for kids to get sick." As soon as I read that message, something didn't feel right in my spirit. I then heard the whisper of the Holy Spirit: *"By whose definition of normal?"*

In that moment, I had an awakening. I realized that it's so easy to lower my expectations and my faith to, "Of course, kids get sick when they go to daycare because it's a germ fest and it builds their immune system." While that's what the world says, is that the reality I am going to live by? In that moment, the Holy Spirit began to convict and challenge me—what normal am I going to live by? What the world or even science or medicine says? Or am I going to live by the higher reality that has been purchased for me by Jesus, into Whom I am grafted, so I have access to all the promises of Scripture? One of those being Psalm 91:10: *"No harm will overtake you; no illness will come near your home"* (NET). Is that just a nice saying that I can buy on a fridge magnet and put on my fridge? Or is that the Word of God?

A fire of conviction began to burn within me. I am going to do what Bob Jones always said to do: "Take it to the bank." By my faith, I am going to take what is promised to me and my family. In a moment, God awakened me to a new level of normal in little things. I didn't even realize I had aligned my faith and expectations with things that were contrary to the Word of God.

Back to the encounter. As this mighty move of the Spirit and awakening to faith and power of the Word of God was taking place, I saw greater miracles, signs, wonders, and mighty demonstrations of His power taking place on the earth in intensity and acceleration (see Heb. 4:12). I heard Him speak again:

"Now is the time for greater access to what I have written in My books in the library of heaven over individuals, cities, and nations as the faith of My people is increasing. While the chains of doubt remained, insight and clarity of what I am speaking was hindered. But now in this new era as this increase and arising to a 'new level of normal' is taking place, I am raising up an army, My army, branded with the fire of the conviction of Matthew 19:26: 'With God *all* things are possible.'"

Looking straight into their eyes, Jesus replied, "Humanly speaking, no one, because no one can save himself. But what seems impossible to you is never impossible to God!" (Matthew 19:26 TPT)

This new era is being branded with Matthew 19:26—the impossible looking completely possible in Jesus. Think about salvation. *"While we were still sinners, Christ died for us"* (Rom. 5:8). He made a way where there was no way; now we walk in Him and by Him and in His authority to see the impossible become possible, not because of our human strength but because of His power. This is the era when we will see the greatest demonstrations of impossibilities bow to the name of Jesus on a scale we have never seen. The glorious awakening to the power in the name of Jesus will sweep the earth far and wide, declaring the truth that He is Lord, and one day every knee will bow and tongue confess that He is God (see Phil. 2:10-11).

Many of you, especially in the last decade, have walked through some of the most difficult seasons of your life. There have been so many battles, assaults, dark nights, and blazing fires, but through it all He has been with you, holding you, encouraging you, loving you, and strengthening you. He has been doing a work deep within you that you may not even realize, and now in this new era He is moving you out of the realm of disappointment and into the place of breakthrough, empowerment, strength, and maturity.

God is looking for those who will partner with His Spirit and be people of the Word, who not only *know* the Word but *live* the Word and walk *on* the Word and in obedience to it by faith. This new era is going to see the people of God take bold steps of faith and see the mountains moved. We cannot partner with the Lord in all He is going to do in this new era if we are living from the ground as a chicken, living by the natural realm, tossed to and fro, and living in fear. Those who embrace the move of His Spirit and His maturing and who live in the Word by *faith* will be like the eagles, soaring in the high places, living in victory.

Can I encourage you to take some time and ask the Holy Spirit if there are any areas of your life where you have been tolerating things lower than all that is yours in Christ? God used a text message to awaken me to a new level of normal—to not expect that "kids just get sick," but to pull me into the higher realm of the promise of Psalm 91:10. Ask the Holy Spirit if there are any areas in your heart and life, and if He reveals any, repent for lowering your faith and ask for His truth and let the Holy Spirit minister to your heart and encourage you in your faith.

"While You Live in the Whys, You Will Not Fly!"

I heard the Lord speaking over the body of Christ recently: *"While you live in the whys, you will not fly."*

I was suddenly taken into a vision. I saw Jesus standing before the people of God, and He was inviting them into new directions in this new era, new pathways, new adventures, new levels of exploration and faith, and He had His hand outstretched.

As the invitation was before them, I heard many people saying things like, "*But why* did this happen Lord? *But why* did that happen?" I then looked at their eyes and they had sunglasses on, and on their sunglasses was written the word *disappointment*. Everything that they were looking at was being viewed through the lens of disappointment.

What struck me strongly in that vision was that these were sunglasses, and they could be *taken off*. It was a *choice* to wear them. It was a choice to stay disappointed. This really struck me because it reminded me of the deep pain that I have felt in many seasons past when disappointment has almost suffocated the life out of me. As I pondered this thought while watching the vision take place, I heard First Samuel 30:6:

> *And David was greatly distressed, for the people spoke of stoning him, because all the people were bitter in soul, each for his sons and daughters But David strengthened himself in the Lord* (ESV).

As I heard that Scripture loudly in this vision, I was surrounded by this strong thought. It doesn't say, "David was slightly upset." It says, "David was *greatly distressed*." Why? He had lost his two wives and people spoke of stoning him. Why? Because the people were bitter in soul.

I stopped and pondered for a second. David in that moment had every right to have a meltdown. David had every right in the natural to be in fear, to be incredibly discouraged and it says he *was* greatly distressed, but did he stop there? No! He made a decision in that moment to "strengthen himself in the Lord." David rose above what was going on in his soul.

The Lord spoke to me in this vision as I looked into the eyes of Jesus. I saw compassion—deep compassion for the pain and for the weariness that many have faced, but in His eyes I also saw a longing. It was a longing for His people to take His hand and—through their faith, through their free will, through their ability to choose—to not live in the disappointment anymore. To take His hand and choose to believe again.

I remember thinking in this vision, "Lord, disappointment is so heavy, it's so caging, it's hard to come out of it. It's your Spirit who brings the healing of disappointment." I heard the Lord say: *"Look away from the disappointment. Lay down the whys, lay down the buts, and take off the sunglasses that are blocking the view of the Son."* It was a decision of the heart that says, "I am not going to live there anymore. I am not going to hold on to this anymore. I am going to bring my center back to Jesus."

I understood what the Lord was saying then. It was about *focus*. It was the place of, "What am I focusing on? What am I rehearsing?" If I am rehearsing the whys and the buts, then I am not going to run in this new era; I am going to remain stuck.

What did it look like for David to encourage himself in the Lord?

[He] took all patiently, and exercised faith on his God; he encouraged himself in the power and providence of God; in the promises of God, and his faithfulness in keeping them; in a view of his covenant relation to God; in remembrance of the grace, mercy, and goodness of God, and his former experiences of it; hoping and believing that God would appear for him in some way or another, and work salvation for him. The Targum is, "he strengthened himself in the Word of the Lord his God;" in Christ the Word of God, and in the power of His might, and in the grace that is in him (Ephesians 6:10, 2 Timothy 2:1).[2]

David looked past the natural circumstances and looked to God. This is the call of maturity that the Lord is placing upon the body of Christ now as we move further into this new era. We cannot be people who are led by our souls.

In this vision I knew that the healing, the grace, the anointing, the freedom was coming in the place of the "letting go." There was a "double-mindedness" in the heart that was saying to Jesus, "I cannot come with You into the new, I cannot take Your hand again, I can't trust You again because I don't understand why 'x, y, z' happened to me." Jesus wasn't asking His people not to feel pain; He wasn't saying "don't grieve" or "get over it." But there was a very strong sense in my vision of, "Unless I get the answers to the *whys*, I am not moving; I can't move."

It was an invitation in this encounter to remove alignment from disappointment, take off the glasses, and look at Him again. To encourage themselves in the Lord and not doubt who He is but *remind* themselves again of who He is—that He is faithful, He never lies, He never fails, He's always the same. He is always working for our good. He is always taking us from glory to glory. What the enemy meant for harm, God will turn for good.

The only way I can describe the atmosphere in this encounter was that the love of Jesus for His people was strongly inviting them to *decide*—am I going to run again by taking Him at His Word, or am I going to stay stuck in my soul? God is healing disappointment, and in this new era we are moving from the place of *"Hope deferred makes the heart sick"* into the *"but a dream fulfilled is a tree of life"* (Prov. 13:12 NLT).

My friend Jason Hooper, senior pastor of Kingsway Church in Alabama, shared a revelation with me recently that God gave him that is completely where we are right now:

> 2020 will be a year of what we have seen and said we are about to taste and see. A decade of disappointment has come to an end and a decade of declaration with demonstration has begun. I feel like many in the body of Christ have been in a Proverbs 13:12 holding pattern where hope deferred has made the heart sick but a desire fulfilled is a tree of life and New Year's Eve 2019, January 1, 2020 we crossed over the big "but." We went from the deferment of hope right into desire fulfilled.

I want you to receive that word today, friend. You are no longer in the holding pattern of the first half of Proverbs 13:12 where hope has been deferred, that decade of disappointment, but you have now moved into the decade of declaration with demonstration. God is awakening us to the power of our decree *by faith* and then seeing the mighty demonstrations of His power to fulfill His Word.

This encounter where I saw Jesus leading His people out of disappointment, bringing healing, and making a choice to not live there anymore opened up to them a whole new realm and world of possibility, expectancy, and faith. Hope being restored again.

God's desire is to move the Church from *defense* to *offense*. We have to be people who are walking in the offense rather than defense. Living led by our soul will cause us to always live on the defense. Living in the revelation of who He is and His Word, how He sees, and what He speaks *by faith* will cause us to live on the *offense*. You are not fighting *for* victory; you are fighting *from* it.

The Giant of Fear

Fear is the opposite of faith. Faith is trust; fear causes us to run and withdraw if we agree and align with it. God spoke something so profound to me regarding the giant of fear in this new era: *"If you are in fear of this new era, you won't slay the giant of fear."*

When He spoke that, it made total sense to me. If you or I are living in the place of fear of this new era and what it entails, what it requires, what will happen, etc. and we choose to put our faith and agreement in that place of fear, then we will not slay the giant of fear that will come against us.

One of the giants that will need to be slain in this new era is the giant of fear because we are moving in uncharted territory. There will be fear of the unknown, fear of stepping out, fear of man, fear of rejection, etc., and if we bow to and align with those areas of fear that raise their ugly heads to stop us from taking the new territories, then we will not slay the giants that stand before our promised lands.

Fear is always something that believers will battle, but the Lord showed me that the enemy is going to come with fear in intensity in this new era, so we are to be prepared. That's where we live in *bold* faith. That's where we remind ourselves who is for us, who is with us, greater is He who is within us, and that God does not give us a spirit of fear but of power and love and a sound mind (see Rom. 8:31; 1 John 4:4; 2 Tim. 1:7).

The increasing revelation of Jesus Christ and the power of the Word of God will increase in believers who embrace the work of the

Holy Spirit. In this great maturing, they are going to *slay* the giants of fear. They will be the Davids, who will arise as men and women after God's own heart with the stones of revelation in their hands, knowing who their God is. They will stand before the giants and declare as David did in First Samuel 17:26:

> For who is this uncircumcised Philistine, that he should defy the armies of the living God? (ESV)

That roar of faith rooted in the revelation of the nature and love of God is going to come out of believers living as friends of God, louder than we have ever heard it. They will stand with fire and conviction and declare over situations that are opposite to what God is speaking, "Who do you think you are, attempting to defy the Word of God and what the Lord is speaking?"

This is a people who live in and from their seat. A people who govern from their seat. A people who see Him and see the Word of the Lord and what He is speaking and move on it by faith, unshakeable, unstoppable, knowing that He will accomplish that which He has spoken and who will tolerate nothing less than what He has promised (see Isa. 55:11). Giants and fear may come, but these ones are so consumed by the revelation of Jesus and who He is and His authority that they see not the problem before them but Jesus the *answer*.

The perspective shift to greater realms of faith is and will continue to take place. A bold people will arise in the earth like never before. I don't stand and live in the natural realm, but I live by every Word that flows from His mouth (see Matt. 4:4). If I live there, then I am unstoppable. If I live there, then I am not caged in fear. If I live in the place of relationship with Him where I am hearing what He is saying and feasting on the Word, filling my heart with truth, *that* frames every part of my life. I position myself in faith and expectation that God is not a liar; He is faithful and will do what He says He will do. It may look different from what I expect or when I expect it to happen, but the way He moves is always greater than my expectation (see Eph. 3:20).

God is raising up a people with fortified, strong, mature faith muscles. Those who have been through the fire and remained. Those who have their roots in one thing alone—Jesus Christ. The One who never changes. The One who is the same yesterday, today, and forever.

The ferocious focus of faith. It's not hard. It's simple.

Keep your eyes in one place—locked with His. When you see Jesus and look into His eyes, you'll see that He is the answer. He is the Word, and when you *believe* what you see, nothing will be impossible for you.

Notes

1.   Kenneth Copeland, "Three Ways to Overcome Unbelief," kcm.org, March 20, 2018, https://blog.kcm.org/3-ways -overcome-unbelief.

2.   *John Gill's Exposition of the Bible*, 1 Samuel 30:6, accessed April 19, 2020, https://www.biblestudytools.com/commentaries/gills -exposition-of-the-bible/1-samuel-30-6.html.

Chapter Ten

I HEARD THE LORD SAY "I AM WEIGHING YOUR WORDS"

I write this chapter as we have entered the year of 5780 according to the Hebrew calendar. The Hebrew letter for 80 is *peh*. It is also the Hebrew word for "mouth." This is an era when the Lord is teaching the body of Christ in greater ways the power of our words and the power of His decree in our mouth. It is an invitation to walk in a realm of faith where the body of Christ understands our authority in Christ at a greater level than we have before, and it is a time of seeing what we decree. In this new era, we will see a greater manifestation of Job 22:28:

*You will also decree a thing, and it will be established for
you; and light will shine on your ways* (NASB).

Other translations use the word *decide*:

*You will decide on a matter, and it will be established for
you, and light will shine on your ways* (ESV).

It is a time to decide what we believe. It's a time to decide where we
put our faith. To decide if we walk in the natural realm, governed by
our circumstances, or if we live and govern from our seat in heavenly
places (see Eph. 2:6).

There are other places within this book where I discuss the call
to walk by faith, to walk in our authority in the power of God manifested in the earth like never before, and to see the power of the Word
of God manifest in ways that we have never seen or imagined before.
The Lord is leading us as His people to the place where we shall see the
power of our words more than ever before. The power that words have
in our lives to create, to build up, or to tear down. Ephesians 4:29 says:

*Let no corrupting talk come out of your mouths, but only
such as is good for building up, as fits the occasion, that it
may give grace to those who hear* (ESV).

*Let no unwholesome word proceed from your mouth, but
only such a word as is good for edification according to the
need of the moment, so that it will give grace to those who
hear* (NASB).

The God who created the earth by what He spoke, by His Word, is
going to take the Church to a place of greater awakening to what takes
place in the spirit when we speak. Psalm 33:9 says:

For he spoke, and it came to be; he commanded, and it stood firm (ESV).

Our glorious Jesus by one word commanded the wind and the waves to be still and they did:

When Jesus woke up, he rebuked the wind and said to the waves, "Silence! Be still!" Suddenly the wind stopped, and there was a great calm (Mark 4:39 NLT).

Matthew 28:18 says we have been given all authority in Christ. We are moving into a time when we are going to see the manifestation of His power, signs, wonders, and miracles take place when we decree that which He speaks. He is dealing with unbelief in the hearts of His people in this new era and leading us into a place of greater faith and trust in Him. There are so many examples in Scripture of the power of the spoken Word of God, from Joshua commanding the sun to stand still for three days (see Josh. 10:12), to Peter in Acts 3:6 commanding the lame man to rise up and walk, to Jesus speaking the word and the centurion's servant being healed (see Matt. 8:8).

There is going to be such a major increase of creative miracles in this new era that will manifest through the power of decree in Jesus' name. Speaking out the Word of God and the promises of Scripture by faith, calling things that are not as though they were (see Rom. 4:17), and seeing a greater accelerated manifestation of the word spoken in the natural. We will see a greater demonstration of the authority of Christ manifesting in the natural through the power of the spoken word. Not only will this take place on an individual basis in the life of a believer but also on a corporate level in the body of Christ and then on a global scale in the earth. We have had little foretastes of this in miracles we have already seen in the Church, individually and in the earth, but the Lord showed me that we haven't even scratched the surface of what is going to come. Shifts will take place in the earth through the decree of His Word through a people who refuse to move from the Word of God and the *rhema* words that are flowing from His mouth (see Matt. 4:4).

Because of the magnitude of what we are moving into in the realm of decreeing the Lord's Word and its manifestation, God is beginning to take the Church through a purification and preparation. I would even use the term "greater training" in the words that are spoken from the mouths of believers.

I had an encounter with the Lord at the beginning of 2020, and I saw the Lord sitting on the throne and He had a large book before Him. He was looking through this book very carefully, page by page, and as I watched I could feel the fear of the Lord strongly. It was then that I heard the words: *"I am weighing the words of My people in this hour."*

Instantly, I knew in the spirit this book contained the words spoken by God's people. It wasn't just some of their words—it was all of their words. I suddenly began to think of all the times when I had used careless words or I had thrown words around that were not life-giving. I remember repenting for any words that I had spoken that were idle or careless words. The Lord began to convict me many years ago about the careless words that I would throw around: "Oh, I am sick and tired of that," or, "I can't handle this anymore"—words that I thought were just communicating my frustrations or stress. But the Lord began to show me more and more the power of the spoken word and how life and death is in the power of the tongue, and I began to be a lot more careful in what I proclaimed over my life. Proverbs 18:21 surrounded me:

Death and life are in the power of the tongue, and those who love it will eat its fruits (ESV).

Your words are so powerful that they will kill or give life, and the talkative person will reap the consequences (TPT).

I remember many years ago when the Lord spoke to me that the greatest prophet over my life was me. It challenged me deeply—what am I speaking over my own life? What am I actually creating in the spirit over my life by what I speak? So in all that I speak, I want to be creating and building in the Spirit what God is speaking over my life. It brought me to a deeper place of specifically asking the Lord what He was speaking over my life, my marriage, my family, my future, etc. Then, through the Word, through dreams, through visions and encounters the Lord began to show me more and more what He was speaking, and I would then align myself with His decree over my life and continue to speak it, *knowing* that whatever word He speaks would not return void (see Isa. 55:11)

Welcome to the School of the Mouth

I remember in November 2019 having a deep encounter with the Lord. Over this decade of declaration, I heard the Lord whisper, "*Welcome to the school of the mouth.*"

It was a beautiful invitation to be schooled by Him in deeper ways in what we speak, which would lead to a realm of revelation of reintroduction to the power of decree and the authority and power of the Word of God. The sense surrounded me strongly that in this move of God we are going to be entrusted with a weighty responsibility as the people of God to steward our words well. The Holy Spirit spoke again:

> "Fire is coming upon the tongue. I am bringing *major* deliverance to My people of *wrong* declarations."

There is a *major* purification and conviction of the Holy Spirit coming into the body of Christ like we have never seen before to bring conviction and purification of words that are spoken. For the Lord is going to bring forth *deep* healing in the hearts of many as they say *yes* to entering into the school of the mouth with the Lord. *"For out of the abundance of the heart the mouth speaks"* (Matt. 12:34).

The Lord is going to continue to convict and highlight words that are flowing out of mouths that are not in line with the Word of God and the truth of Scripture. It is the love of God that is going to bring the correction. He is going to the root of lies, unforgiveness, bitterness, and the place of "careless speech" as He trains His people in the power of words and the power in the tongue, because we are moving into a time when we will decree what the Lord is saying and there shall be a *sudden* manifestation.

When the Lord spoke, *"Fire is coming upon the tongue,"* He spoke of conviction and purification, but He also spoke of commissioning. This is the era when fire will fall upon tongues and a greater commissioning will take place of those being positioned to speak, sing, and declare the Word of the Lord. Many have lost their voice, and this is the era when voices will be restored.

There is a mighty wave of His deliverance being released upon the tongue to deliver the people of God from declaring things that are not His heart, not what He is saying, and not His truth. God is dealing with lies and half-truths and leading His people into a place of declaring what He is saying and aligning with His Word.

Heavenly Wisdom

I heard the Lord say, *"Those who embrace the school of the mouth will have mouths that flow with heavenly wisdom that has never been seen before."* By His Spirit, the Lord is going to take us through intense training, purifying, and preparation in the school of the mouth. We will see *major* revelation and impartation of wisdom being released to us. We shall open our mouths and out shall flow revelation of His wisdom and the mind of Christ that has not been seen before. The level of wisdom God is going to release will be unprecedented.

It's all about yielding to the process and training of the Lord to speak what He sees and then see the manifestation of what He speaks. The Lord showed me that many are speaking words of death over their lives, not words of life, and there is a mighty heralding summons of the Lord to stand in this new era and to speak *only that* which He speaks and to speak *life*.

The Lord is going to demonstrate like *never before* in this new era the power of words and the power of *blessing* and decreeing His Word. Positions of authority and influence in the earth will increase to speak that which He is saying.

> *For if you keep silent at this time, relief and deliverance will rise for the Jews from another place, but you and your father's house will perish. And who knows whether you have not come to the kingdom for such a time as this?* (Esther 4:14 ESV)

In this Esther, Joseph, and Daniel era there will be ever-increasing doors that are going to open to many in the body of Christ to move into different mountains of culture to speak forth the Word of the Lord. This invitation into the school of the mouth with the Lord is going to see these ones receive the wisdom and download of blueprint strategies from heaven to answer the problems and issues that kings and leaders will need. We have seen this has already begun, but it is going to increase in momentum like we have never seen before. The Church will be called on to *speak* the wisdom of God in places of significant influence that will shift and change nations.

The Spirit is delivering His people from wrong declarations that are rooted in lies and not the truth of His Word. Through the declaration and decree of His Word in prayer, there will be *mighty* deliverance in cities and nations both to those of influence and those leading the mountains of culture. I heard the Lord say:

> "In this new era there will be mighty demonstrations of My decrees suddenly unlocking the destiny in nations in ways that have never been seen before. *Watch the deliverance* that will take place in the decree of My Word in prayer."

There is about to be an *explosive* demonstration of the deliverance of God that will be seen in prayer and intercession as the Word of God is decreed and declared. In this decade of decree and declaration there will be *powerful* demonstrations of the power of decreeing the Word of God—sudden shifts and manifestations will happen in accelerated momentum. These powerful demonstrations will not just be sporadic and "here or there," but it will become the norm to see swift shifts and answered prayer through the decree of His Word.

Coming out of that encounter with the Lord, I was blown away again by the magnitude of what God is going to do in this new era and the privilege we have been given to be alive at this time. This was a beautiful invitation and a weighty warning that He was releasing for us as we move in this new era.

I began this chapter by sharing with you the Lord saying, *"I am weighing your words."* I want to continue to share with you what I saw. I watched the Lord read through all the words spoken out of the mouths of His people, and I felt the weighty fear of the Lord and the reminder from His Spirit that life and death are in the power of the tongue (see Prov. 18:21; James 3:1-12). Matthew 12:36 began to thunder in my heart:

> *And I tell you this, you must give an account on judgment day for every idle word you speak* (NLT).

The Lord then spoke to me:

> **"There is a mighty wave of conviction by My Spirit coming upon My people in this new era for idle words that have been spoken. For My people to move into all that I have for them in this new era, they must move away from speaking idle words and careless words. I am raising up an army who have swords in their mouths, and the only sword that should be in their mouths is the sword of My Word."**

Then suddenly the vision changed and I saw many believers and they had swords in their mouths. Sword after sword would leave their mouths and cut people down at the knees, and then other swords would leave their mouths and would stab people in the back. Other swords would leave their mouths and stab others in the heart. Then the next minute they would be speaking the Word of God and have the sword of the Word in their mouth. Then they would suddenly turn another way and the sword in their mouth was the sword that cut others down.

I was shocked. These were believers. These were words being spoken by believers over other believers. They were words spoken behind the backs of others. These were words spoken in secret. These were word curses spoken over one another. These were poisonous words. The Lord spoke again:

> "I am grieved by the words that are being spoken by many in My Church. There are such poisonous words being spoken amongst My people and I see every word. I hear every word, and many are living with two swords in their mouth. They are decreeing My Word, but then they are using their words to tear down and speak death over one another."

The sense surrounded me so strongly that this conviction of the Holy Spirit that's coming in this new era is going to bring forth a great restoration of the fear of God over the words being spoken and thrown around in the body of Christ. As the Lord spoke: *"I am raising up an army who have swords in their mouths, and the only sword that should be in their mouths is the sword of My Word."*

Careless Whispers

The Lord continued to speak: *"There are many careless whispers leaving the mouths of believers against one another, but conviction is coming against these whispers as in this new era I am bringing forth a unity in My Church that is deeper than has been."*

It reminded me of a dream I had a few years ago. In the dream I was in a church and I was standing before a lady who had cancer and she wanted me to pray for her. We were talking about her condition and she said to me, "It's so sad that the word *cancer* is on so many believers' lips," and I agreed. Then suddenly the church we were in began to shake violently and the roof began to crack when a *huge* tidal wave crashed into the church. It was engulfing everyone in the church and I knew that this wave was coming and bringing healing and cancer was losing its hold in the lives of believers, and I woke up.

As I sat with the Lord journaling the dream, I was so excited regarding this mighty wave of His healing that was going to crash into the Church in an exponential way, to see cancer lose its hold like never before. Then the Holy Spirit whispered to me, *"Lana, this is a twofold dream. It also has another meaning."* So, I asked the Lord what the second layer was. He took me straight back to the sentence that came out of the mouth of the lady with cancer. She said, "It's so sad that the word *cancer* is on so many believers' lips." Suddenly the understanding came to me. The Lord was showing through this dream that there was indeed a healing wave increasing in the Church to see cancer defeated on a greater mass scale than we had seen, but the Lord was also speaking about the "cancer" on people's lips—the death that was on the lips of His people. He was speaking about words—the words of death that are on the lips of His people.

I was taken back into the dream, but in a vision, and I saw the wave crashing into the church again through the roof. As I saw the wave crash in, I heard the words, "Be washed with the water of the Word" (see Eph. 5:26), and I knew there was a great cleansing that was coming to the Church in the area of the words spoken. The Lord was inviting the people of God to be washed and convicted by the Word of God, especially in the area of speech.

In the area of words spoken over our own lives and over the lives of others, a mighty fire of His purifying, purging, and convicting is going to increase upon the body of Christ. Those who embrace the increasing conviction of the Holy Spirit will be matured in their speech. They will demonstrate in integrity the power of decreeing the Word of God over others.

The Lord is going to deal with the backbiting, the jealous words, the cutting one another down, the lack of authenticity, the word curses, and the daggers being thrown around the body of Christ. He will mature the Church in greater ways into those who truly love one another; those who truly would lay down their lives for their brothers; those who embrace, encourage, and celebrate one another, considering others as better than themselves (see John 13:34-35; 15:13; 1 Thess. 5:11; Phil. 2:3). This will come through deep conviction of the Holy Spirit and the Word and our awakening to His love and our identity as His sons and daughters. The correction of God—dealing with words being spoken behind backs, behind closed doors, the lack of honor, and poison being sent forth through swords in believers' mouths—is all out of His love. His heart is to bring the Church into a greater place of John 17, that we should be known by *our love.* How shall we be known by our love if there is so much backbiting, poison, and disunity among His armies who are meant to fight and stand as one in *love?*

Out of the Heart the Mouth Speaks

I remember many years ago when I opened up the fridge to get something and the milk fell out. It crashed to the ground, spilling liters of milk everywhere. I turned to Kevin and I said, "Of course that would happen to me." Kevin looked at me with a look that said a thousand words. He didn't even have to open his mouth; I knew exactly what was happening in that moment. Not only did Kevin pick up on what was going on, but I also felt the Holy Spirit convicting my heart. I felt the gentle nudge of His loving conviction asking me a question, and it wasn't "Why did you *say* that?" it was "Why do you *believe* that?" See, there was a belief that had taken root in my heart that wasn't from God or in line with what the Word says, and I had allowed it to land and bear fruit in my heart.

The Holy Spirit was revealing to me that clearly there was a lie that I was believing and had aligned with, and the overflow of that fruit in my heart was coming out of my mouth (see Luke 6:45). So I stepped aside and I began to ask the Holy Spirit what was going on in my heart, and sure enough He revealed to me the lie that had taken root in my heart because of situations I had walked through over the years. What I believed affected what I spoke and expected. My expectation wasn't faith; it wasn't life—it was, in essence, "Bad things always happen to me."

So in our journey of "watching our words" and being people whose mouths are filled with decrees of His Word, we have to be people whose hearts are feasting upon the Word of God, the *living* Word of God (see Heb. 4:12), and filling our hearts with His truth. What we put into our hearts is ultimately what is going to come out of our mouths. *Your words will reveal what is in your heart.*

Watching our words is so important and also is a very clear indicator of what is happening in our hearts. God wants you and me walking in the awakening and revelation of the power of our words and the power to create and shift atmospheres and see impossibilities come tumbling down because of the authority that we carry in Christ as people *of* the Word. I heard the Lord say recently:

> **"My people are to be people of the *Word* and not the *world*."**

I appeal to you therefore, brothers, by the mercies of God, to present your bodies as a living sacrifice, holy and acceptable to God, which is your spiritual worship. Do not be conformed to this world, but be transformed by the renewal of your mind, that by testing you may discern what is the will of God, what is good and acceptable and perfect (Romans 12:1-2 ESV).

I want to focus on a few words in that verse: "Do not be conformed to this world, but be transformed by the renewal of your mind." Why am I talking about renewing your mind in a chapter about watching your words?

Renewing your mind is *key* to your decree. In this new era there is an invitation to walk in the mind of Christ and wisdom of God in unprecedented ways. There is a line being drawn in the sand by the hand of God, which is such a weighty invitation, and that invitation is the invitation to *decide and align* with the Word of God.

In the Holy Spirit's dealings in the lives of believers concerning their words and their hearts, the Lord is going to be revealing areas of the heart where the revelation of the Word of God has not taken deep root. The Lord is inviting us into a deep place in the Word of God, where our hearts are bubbling and overflowing with the Word of God day and night, not just on a Sunday. The Lord is calling the Church to walk in a level of faith in the revelation of His Word that we have not yet walked in.

Focus and Intentionality: Renewing of the Mind

We are coming deeper into this new era of walking in and working out Second Corinthians 10:5, coupled with Romans 12:2 that we looked at above.

> *We destroy arguments and every lofty opinion raised against the knowledge of God, and take every thought captive to obey Christ* (ESV).

There is an urgency to steward the Word of God in our hearts and in our minds in this new era. The only way I have been able to describe it is a *focus* that is required in this new era to walk in *intentionality* in the words that come out of our mouths and the renewing of our mind. The Lord showed me that these are two keys that are going to be needed for what He is going to do in this new era. Bill Johnson says, "You know your mind is renewed when the impossible looks logical."

What we are moving into in the realm of faith and the miraculous in this new era is going to be carried and released through a people whose minds are renewed to the revelation of who Jesus is, who they are in Him, and the power of His Word. There is a mighty attack of distraction that has been assaulting the body of Christ and will continue to remove God's people from the *ferocious focus of faith.* God is calling His people into intentionality in the realm of faith. The place that says, "My God said it, end of story! I am not moving." It's the place of living in such deep revelation of who Jesus is and encounter with Him daily as we live on earth as "visitors." We see as He sees and we move by what He speaks, not what the natural realm dictates to us.

The Lord spoke to me recently, and He said, *"It's time for My people to be led by My Spirit like never before and divorce being led by their soul."*

It's Time for a Deeper Place of Dedication

There was a roar that came over me in that moment. It was the *roar* of the Lord in victory, calling His people into a place of decision. It was calling the people of God into the place where they had to make a decision in this new era. It was the call of faith. It was a call of consecration in this new era to the Lord, and part of that consecration was being set apart from anything that is contrary or stands against the Word of the Lord. God is calling His people in this new era to a place of *dedication*.

Merriam-Wester's Dictionary defines *dedication* as "a devoting or setting aside for a particular purpose; commitment, allegiance, faithfulness, constancy." Part of this dedication, I believe, is the resolve of taking the Lord at His Word. The weariness, the length of the battle, discouragement, hopelessness, complacency, sinful desires, fear, and wounding have brought about a "double-mindedness" in the Church that the Lord is going to uproot in this new era. It is out of His love that He is going to be shaking and awaking the Church to come to a place where the Word of the Lord is the only option. Where what He speaks becomes the true reality like never before. He is such a loving Father, He is such a good Father, that He wants His people walking in victory and overcoming in levels and realms that the Church hasn't before.

The Lord showed me that there has been a "drifting away" that has taken place over many years in the body of Christ from the place of deep-rooted, single-minded focus upon the Lord and His Word to entertaining a double-mindedness. James 1:5-8 says:

> *If any of you lacks wisdom, let him ask God, who gives gen-*
> *erously to all without reproach, and it will be given him.*
> *But let him ask in faith, with no doubting, for the one who*
> *doubts is like a wave of the sea that is driven and tossed by*
> *the wind. For that person must not suppose that he will*
> *receive anything from the Lord; he is a double-minded man,*
> *unstable in all his ways* (ESV).

This is the era when we will see the greatest signs, wonders, and miracles that have ever been seen. This is the era of the greatest unveiling of the wisdom of God in the earth we have ever seen.

What you focus on, what you place in your heart, what you feed on, what you believe, how you walk in this new era with a renewed mind—walking in the mind of Christ or walking in the natural realm—all plays a huge part in what you speak and what you decree.

Let's Do Some Homework

I want to give you some homework for this chapter.

1. I want to encourage you to *sit with the Lord and write out Scriptures and decrees* for this new era. Ask the Lord what He is saying and what it is that He wants you to decree. Ask Him what His heart is, what His plans are, His blueprints, His revelations, and set up your boundary lines with the Word of God.

2. *Ask the Holy Spirit to examine your heart.* Are there any areas of unbelief, any areas of doublemindedness, and any times when you have spoken words over yourself or others that have been not in line with what He is speaking and His Word? This is not to condemn—the

Lord does not condemn—but this is to "clean the slate." I encourage you to repent as the Lord highlights these things. It's not a once-off thing; I encourage you to keep short accounts with the Lord on the words you are speaking. Ask the Holy Spirit to continually guide your words and what you speak as you listen to His voice and fill your heart with His Word.

3. *Decree daily*. Make it a part of your daily routine. Set up a reminder on your phone or put the Word of God somewhere in your house where you will see it all the time, so you have it continually before you and you are speaking what He is speaking. In 2019, the Lord told me it was time for me to "walk on the Word" like never before. So I wrote the promises of Scripture that the Lord had highlighted on sticky notes and put them in my socks. Sounds weird, hey? But every time I walked, I would feel the sticky note in my socks and it would remind me of His promise and I would speak out His truth and decree His Word.

4. *Ask the Lord how you can love and encourage others* through your words and spur them on in faith.

> *Let us consider how to stir up one another to love and good works, not neglecting to meet together, as is the habit of some, but encouraging one another, and all the more as you see the Day drawing near* (Hebrews 10:24-25 ESV).

However the Lord leads you, I encourage you to invite the Holy Spirit to come and lead you in the area of what you speak over yourself and over others. Allow the conviction of the Holy Spirit to rest upon you if and when it needs to. Allow the Lord to take you deeper in understanding of the power of your words.

This is the era when the body of Christ embraces His pruning, purifying, purging, and awakening to the power of decree and the power of words. We will see mighty demonstrations of Job 22:28:

> *You will also declare a thing, and it will be established for you; so light will shine on your ways.*

Let Proverbs 18:21 be a Scripture that we keep before our eyes in this new era to remind us of the power of our words:

> *Words kill, words give life; they're either poison or fruit— you choose* (MSG).

> *Your words are so powerful that they will kill or give life, and the talkative person will reap the consequences* (TPT).

Let *life* flow from our mouths. Let us be known as the people of God who speak life, love, encouragement, and truth over *all*.

Chapter Eleven

THIS IS YOUR DECADE OF
DELIVERANCE

There is a decree that I believe the Lord wants me to release over you, and it is this: *"This is your decade of deliverance."*

For the last year or so, the Lord has been speaking to me over and over about a mighty wave of deliverance that is increasing in the body of Christ in this new era. He has been speaking to me about the *day* of deliverance that we are in right now. I want you to hear that. It's not a time that's coming; we have entered into it. The major deliverance that is upon the Church is going to be monumental. There has been so much that has held down the body of Christ. There is so much that has attempted to keep God's people bound, and the enemy has been having a "field day" with it because he wants to keep the people of God in chains rather than running in the freedom that has been purchased for us at Calvary through the death and resurrection of our beautiful Jesus. I hear the resounding sound of John 8:36:

> *So if the Son sets you free, you will be free indeed* (ESV).
>
> *So if the Son sets you free from sin, then become a true son and be **unquestionably** free!* (TPT)

I believe in this new era, God is challenging us in whether we believe we are free or not. Let me explain this to you. As I sat and pondered this Scripture before the Lord, I felt the Lord say that there are many who are being swayed in their *belief* in freedom because of their *experience* of freedom.

First and foremost, the context of this verse is our salvation. We are free in Christ because He set us free. Because He paid the price for our freedom. We didn't pay half; we didn't even pay three fourths—He paid it all. So we are free because of what He did.

I love how *The Passion Translation* says it—*unquestionably free.* I want to do what I always do. I want to look at the meaning of that word. The *Cambridge English Dictionary* defines *unquestionable*: "obvious and impossible to doubt." Look at that for a second. Your freedom cannot be doubted or disputed, and it is without question.

I want you to hear that today. You are unquestionably free in Christ, so we believe it, we live it, we walk in it, and we move in it as we live, move, and have our being in Him. It's a spiritual reality. It's a Kingdom truth. He has set you free and the Lord wants the Church to walk in the greater revelation of that freedom that has been purchased in this new era. I had a vision and I saw many in the body of Christ in the valley of indecision and double-mindedness. They were living in a place of double-mindedness because of their experience: "I know the Bible says I am free. I know the Bible says I am free from sin and death, but I don't see the freedom of Christ manifesting in my life, so maybe I am not truly free."

The Lord showed me that there are many questions in the hearts of believers because of their experiences that have caused them to *question* and *doubt* their freedom. There are going to be *powerful* encounters with Jesus in this new era that are going to *reawaken* the *revelation* of *freedom*. It is going to shake and wake the Church up to the *freedom* that has been purchased for them at Calvary.

I see a few major things happening in the area of freedom in this new era.

1. The awakening to the revelation of identity and freedom in Christ and major demonstrations of that freedom taking place.

2. The empowerment to walk in freedom and demonstration of Christ's freedom in our lives like never before.

There are many who have been battling strongholds, sickness, disease, temptations, addictions, sin, torment, lies, rejections, fears, and many other things for so many years and have not seen breakthrough and the manifestation of the freedom of Christ in their lives. This is the decade of deliverance, when a mighty demonstration of His power will be seen to suddenly and instantly deliver many.

The restoration of the fear of the Lord to the Church will also be one of the ways that the Lord blossoms freedom in the body of Christ, for there will be a holy awe and wonder of who He is, the King of kings and Lord of lords, that will fall upon the Church. It will bring the greatest level of consecration and turning away from sin that we have ever seen, leading the people of God who embrace the move of His Spirit to walk in freedom in unprecedented ways.

God's heart is for His people to occupy. It is time for us to occupy the land that has been promised to us. What He has decreed is ours. In a recent encounter I had with the Lord, I saw the lands where the most ferocious battles have taken place for many. No matter how much they have stood, battled, decreed, and fought to take the land that is theirs in Christ, the battle continued to rage fiercer and fiercer. It has been seemingly never-ending. That's where the word came to me that this is the "day" (decade) of deliverance. I remember hearing Amos 9:14-15 resounding loudly:

> *"They'll rebuild their ruined cities. They'll plant vineyards and drink good wine. They'll work their gardens and eat fresh vegetables. And I'll plant them, plant them on their own land. They'll never again be uprooted from the land I've given them." God, your God, says so* (MSG).

Fortifying and Occupying

There is a fortifying and occupying that God is going to bring in this new era for many, and there will be great blessing and increase awaiting those who seek the Lord. There is a huge harvest waiting in these lands, and that's why the battle has been so fierce for many. There will be new anointings, new mantles that will be walked in, waiting in these lands. The very thing that the enemy has used to try to take many of God's people out in past seasons will become the new lands that they will occupy, through partnering with the Lord by faith, receiving the freedom that's already theirs in Christ, and walking out that freedom through obedience to the Word of God.

This is what I want to communicate here. Freedom is intentional. Yes, Jesus has set us free and freedom is already ours in Christ, but we have to be intentional to walk in what is already ours. Not to be double-minded but to walk in faith, believing wholeheartedly that we are unquestionably free. Walking in obedience to the Word and turning away from sin and not using grace as a license to sin. Receiving the forgiveness that is ours in Christ.

Living a life where we continually "sit back and wait" for God to set us free would be a life that's unbalanced. Are there times when God sovereignly moves and sets His people free? Absolutely! But there are also times when the Lord requires us to walk by faith and in obedience to His Word to bring the manifestation of the freedom that is already ours in Christ into the natural.

So in this new era, I believe that God will indeed move sovereignly at times, but I believe there's a weighty call from the Lord to really align our faith with the revelation of our freedom and not cheapen the price God paid for our freedom through any sort of double-mindedness or unbelief. It's time to position ourselves before the Lord, *knowing* that there are new lands and a time of incredible occupying before us, and ask Him to lead us in deeper revelation of our freedom in Christ and then to walk in and from that revelation.

The Lord spoke to me: *"Because many are living double-minded about freedom, they are not walking in the power of their freedom."*

It's Time for Greater Maturity

So much of this new era is about the Lord maturing the saints in faith and what is already theirs in Christ, and the revelation of our freedom is a huge part of that. He's encouraging us as His people to stop putting our faith in *experience* and to put it in *truth*. I hear the Holy Spirit whispering, *"What is your truth? What truth do you live by?"* Can you see the theme that has flowed and will continue to flow through this book? It's the alignment of the heart, because what you *expect* is what you *experience*. God wants to shift our expectation higher into the *heavenly reality* and *biblical truths* as a firm foundation so we will see what we *expect manifest* in line with His Word.

This isn't a blanket statement that everyone in the body of Christ hasn't been living in the place of freedom—that wouldn't be accurate. But I believe the Lord *is* saying that many have been hindered in their freedom and occupying because they have been believing lies and living by experience rather than biblical truths. Our loving Father wants to bring His people deeper into a place of deliverance and freedom in this new era, so He's going after the alignment and belief of the heart.

Invite the Holy Spirit to minister to your heart right now. Ask the Lord for greater revelation of the freedom that is yours in Christ. I want you to pause here and take a minute and let Him speak to you.

This Is the Era of Your Greatest Restoration and Deliverance

I hear the Holy Spirit whispering:

"The greatest restoration and deliverance of your life is upon you now. The divine alignments of My hand are taking place, and I am leading you into a place of deliverance that you have not ever imagined. You are not your past. I am changing the script. You are not going to follow in the patterns of your family before you. You are not going to live in the same places of sin, addiction, chains, and torment. I am bringing you out into a new land. I am bringing you deeper into the revelation of My goodness, My kindness, and My majesty. I am bringing you deeper into the revelation of your freedom in Me. Get ready for encounters with Me in this new era when you will see the price I paid at the Cross for your deliverance. You will have encounters with Me where the fire of My love and the fire of the power of the Gospel will brand you again, leaving you never the same. You will see My blood that poured out of My side and the nails in My hands; you will see the power of My resurrection again that will leave you in awe and wonder of who I am, My love for you, and My deliverance that was paid for you. I am going to open up the definition of My **sozo** to you. Complete healing, wholeness, deliverance, salvation. Major alignments in your heart and life will take place because of the revelation of My love and freedom that is yours that will burn deep within you. You will weep and weep in thankfulness and joy as you see Me, the One who paid it all because I love you, because you are Mine. This love for you, this revelation of My goodness and freedom will draw you into a life of greater abundance, holiness, purity, deliverance, and freedom. This is the era when you will run with Me unstoppable, victorious, and free like never before. The time has arrived; this is your day of deliverance."

Friend, this is your decade of deliverance and time of divine reset. As I end this chapter, I want to encourage you to take time with the Holy Spirit and invite Him to take you into this place of encounter with Him at the Cross—the death and resurrection of Jesus. Spend time in the Gospels, marinating in the truth of our victorious Jesus who paid it all. There is a divine "second wind" coming upon you to run with the Lord in empowerment like never before.

I am going to leave you here with this prophetic word the Lord gave me for deliverance and strengthening. I felt the Lord wanted me to put this word here as an encouragement to you of the refreshing that's upon you and that will be manifested in this new era. Arising are a people consumed with the revelation of their freedom in Christ and walking in trust for the One whose strong arm brings deliverance.

The Lord spoke to me this week that the enemy has been coming against many to bring about a weariness and to "wear them down." I heard those words repeating over and over in my spirit: "wear them down."

It was like a "grinding down," like adding another weight to the load; it was another hit when they are already wounded, and it has become harder and harder for many to keep standing. So many have been in their times with the Lord crying out, "God, I can't stand anymore. God, where is the reprieve? God, where is the release? I feel so empty and like I am barely surviving."

Those who were in this place feeling so worn down, I heard the Lord say, "The enemy has attempted to wear them down, to bring a weariness that is deeper than they have ever known, but I have seen and I am the God of deliverance; I am the God of perfect timing. My strong arm is bringing deliverance and strengthening. I am thundering over these ones—**empowerment.**"

A New Level of Empowerment

These ones have been worn down to the ground. Emptied. Broken. Hurt. Bruised. Shaken. Wearied. There is a very strong wind of the Spirit, like a hurricane, that is upon these ones that will completely lift them up out of this weariness, out of this place of brokenness, out of this place of despair and hopelessness, and resurrection life will be released into their hearts and into their bodies.

The Lord spoke again: "A new level of empowerment is upon these ones. The enemy has come against them so strongly to weary them and wear them down. Now by the resurrection power of My Spirit they are moving into a new level of **empowerment** of My Spirit. They will experience My power and My Spirit moving in them and through them like never before, and they will stand taller, stronger, and in greater authority than they have. Where the enemy has tried to kill them and steal their authority, in the resurrection power of My Spirit the awakening to the truth that **all** authority is theirs in Christ is being increased."

I then had a vision of these ones so worn down, so broken, the resurrection power of the Spirit had come like a hurricane and brought sudden transformation, restoration, revival, and strengthening. Now they were going further, doing more with the Lord, and seeing greater breakthrough than ever. The Lord thundered over them: *"Expansion!"*

Many of you have been in that place. At the point of giving up. The opposition, the health issues, the financial issues, the marital issues, the attack of witchcraft, lies, fear, and heaviness coming against you, the attack from people, all of it—one thing after another on every side has worn you down. Everything is screaming "*break down,*" but God is decreeing *expansion!*

I heard the Lord say, "The hunted will now become the **hunters!**"

The enemy has hunted you down; he has come at you in every direction, but the Lord is decreeing from heaven, *"Game over!"* The games, the schemes, the wiles of the enemy to break you in this season are *over,* and the Lord is reviving you, strengthening you, and sending you forth and out into greater expansion and increase than you have *ever* known. You are now going out as the *hunter* with Jesus. You are now being set forth by the leading of the Spirit, and you will do great *damage* to the enemy and the kingdom of darkness. The enemy will be *sorry* that he has messed with you. You will be running empowered and in freedom like never before.

Right now, you may feel weaker than you ever have, but in Christ you are about to experience a strength in Him that will manifest in *every area* the enemy has touched in your life to catapult you into a new level of your assignment and destiny in Christ.

The battle has been over what you carry.

This is actually your time of moving into the *fullness of time* in so many ways. The enemy has fought *so* hard to bring delay into your life, but now you are stepping into a fullness you have never known. Watch how things are *suddenly* going to come together and everything and everyone who has taken a stand against you will stand in awe at the resurrection power of Jesus Christ manifested in your life. This *is* your divine comeback!

In all these things we are more than conquerors through Him who loved us (Romans 8:37).

Chapter Twelve

FIRE OF GOD COMING TO THE PROPHETIC STREAM

As we have talked a lot about in this book, this is a time of great alignment, purification, acceleration, and preparation. God is reviving, He is maturing, and He is building. I released a word in November 2019 for the prophets, titled: "Warning to the Prophets in This New Era: Do Not Trade Purity for Platforms."

The Lord is really highlighting stewardship in this new era and purity of heart in the Church. The Lord really does care about heart motives and the "why" behind actions (see

1 Sam. 16:7). For example, there's nothing wrong with posting a photo on Facebook of, let's say, having lunch with someone of great influence, or sharing a testimony of what God has done through you or your ministry. There is a *very* powerful place for sharing testimony, but what I do believe is God is asking us as His people to always ask, *"Why* am I doing this? What is the purpose of this posting?" I believe that the Lord is really raising the standard of conviction of the "why" behind actions because of the self-promotion and striving that is keeping the Church from moving in all God has for them. The refiner's fire is falling in this hour, heavier than we have experienced before.

> But who can endure the day of His coming? And who can
> stand when He appears? For he is like a refiner's fire and like
> launderers' soap (Malachi 3:2).

I heard the Lord say recently: *"This is the day of My dealings."* I want you to hear this: *God is dealing because of the great revealing that's coming.* The revealing of the glory of God, His power and majesty in exponential ways, and the revealing of the sons and daughters of the King.

> For all creation is waiting eagerly for that future day when
> God will reveal who his children really are (Romans 8:19
> NLT).

He is dealing with His Church out of His extravagant love to bring forth the great revealing. This is a constant theme throughout this entire book, because this is the preparation and the posturing for the greatest positioning of God's people in the earth to usher in His Kingdom and glory in marvelous ways.

In all of these "dealings of the Lord," I had an encounter with Him in November 2019, and He gave me a prophetic word of warning to the prophets in this new era, which I want to share with you here. In this encounter, I heard the Lord say, *"Prophets, I am issuing a warning to you. Do not trade purity for platforms. Do not use My voice to build your platforms."*

Instantly, I saw a *parading of pride* that was taking place. "Look at what God has spoken to me! Look at the revelation that the Lord has entrusted me with! Look at the Word I am carrying and the doors God has opened for *me.*"

There was such a strong warning in my spirit from the heart of the Lord to not spiritually prostitute the gifting and come to a place of impurity where the revelation that is being released from the heart of God is being used to build platforms. The Lord continued to speak to me:

> "Lana, I am going to restore the fear of God upon the prophetic movement. Many have become familiar and complacent with the privilege that it is to hear My voice and carry My voice and are being driven by a need to be seen rather than overflowing from the secret place, encountering My heart."

I cannot even put into words the grief that came into my heart. I felt the yearning from His heart as His eyes roamed the earth and continue to roam the earth, looking for those prophets and prophetic voices who will steward His heart with *purity, integrity,* and *humility.*

I want to stop here for a moment. What I don't want you to read in this chapter is any dishonor for prophetic leaders and prophets who have gone before me. I am so thankful for those who have gone before me, and I have received so much teaching, training, and understanding from the mothers and fathers in the prophetic movement. I am so thankful for their example, their lives, and their ministry and the gift that they are to the body of Christ.

I want to put this word into context—God is weighing the prophetic movement, and right now it has been found wanting. So out of His love, He is correcting, aligning, and His refiner's fire is coming to purify and purge.

The Lord continued to speak:

> "Lana, I am not just shifting some things in the prophetic movement; I am *reforming* the prophetic movement."

In this new era, we are going to see the revelation of what God is speaking, revealing, and releasing aligned strongly with the divine strategy of God to build and to build in some unexpected ways and places.

In this encounter I had with the Lord I had a vision, and I saw a line of prophets. The first prophet began to prophesy and release the word of the Lord; then the next one began to prophesy and they prophesied louder than the one next to them. Then the next prophet began to prophesy louder than the second one. Then the next prophet began to prophesy louder than the third one, and it went all the way down the line of twelve prophets. There was a competition of who was going to be heard the loudest. There was a pride in the atmosphere that said, "I have the better word; I got the word first; this is *my* prophetic word."

My heart was gripped that there were many in the prophetic movement who were operating out of this place of pride, competition, and impurity. When the Lord spoke of the warning to the prophets to not use His voice to build their own platforms, I felt the fear of God so strongly. It's a call to all prophets to be staying close to the Lord and allowing the conviction of His Spirit to fall if need be.

In this encounter, as I looked at the line I wondered why there were twelve prophets. Instantly, I thought of the twelve disciples and I thought of how the number 12 in Scripture represented perfect government/rule (see Gen. 49:28; Exod. 24:4; 28:21; Josh. 3:12-13; 4:3; Luke 6:13). Adam F. Thompson and Adrian Beale in their book *The Divinity Code* say that the number 12 also represents divine organization, apostolic fullness, and literally twelve.[1]

There is a divine alignment and His perfect order coming to the prophetic movement unlike we have ever seen before. There is a maturing, organizing, reorganizing, and restructuring coming to the prophetic movement where *Jesus* is the center.

God is bringing a higher standard to the prophetic movement. I heard the Lord say:

> "I am raising up plumb-line prophets to release My words into the body of Christ to bring alignment and correction in this new era, but I am also raising up prophets with pure hearts into the areas of the prophetic movement to bring correction and alignment where spiritual prostitution, perversion, mixture, witchcraft, and competition is festering. I am raising up plumb-line prophets who will call out the *parading* that is taking place in the prophetic movement and in the Church."

It Is Time for a Plumb Line

So what is a plumb line?

> A line with a plumb attached to it, used for finding the depth of water or determining the vertical on an upright surface.[2]

> *For who has despised the day of small things? For these seven rejoice to see the plumb line in the hand of Zerubbabel. They are the eyes of the Lord, which scan to and fro throughout the whole earth* (Zechariah 4:10).

> *Then he showed me another vision. I saw the Lord standing beside a wall that had been built using a plumb line. He was using a plumb line to see if it was still straight. And the Lord said to me, "Amos, what do you see?"*

> *I answered, "A plumb line."*

> *And the Lord replied, "I will test my people with this plumb line. I will no longer ignore all their sins. The pagan shrines of your ancestors will be ruined, and the temples of Israel will be destroyed; I will bring the dynasty of King Jeroboam to a sudden end"* (Amos 7:7-9 NLT).

The time of the plumb line has come for the entire body of Christ, including the prophetic movement. He is also raising up plumb-line prophets to take the Word of the Lord into the prophetic movement, and the Church bringing the corrective words of the Lord, which are always for the purpose of redemption, turning, and exhortation to bring His people into greater alignment. Can you see the love of God so deeply here? He loves His people so much that He comes with a plumb line to correct and align (see Heb. 12:6).

Surely the Lord God does nothing, unless He reveals His secret to His servants the prophets (Amos 3:7).

Look at the definition of plumb line again with me: "finding the depth of water or determining the vertical on an upright surface." The Lord continued to speak in this encounter:

> "There are many prophesying words that tickle ears and will increase their popularity, and it lacks depth. My daughter, do you want to know one of the reasons why many prophetic words haven't come to pass? Because I didn't say them. I am holding many of My prophets to account for the false hope they have led others into by prophesying out of their flesh. The deep secrets of My heart in this new era will be released to My friends. The deep secrets of My heart will be shared with the humble, with those who will linger. I will entrust the *pure streams* of My revelation that will bring corporate transformation, reformation, and shift in the body of Christ and the earth to those who are truly seeking My heart and not getting caught up in the acceleration and building their own platforms."

There was such a thundering call from the heart of God over the prophetic movement to "come back to the first love." I heard the Lord say, *"A dazzling has entered the prophetic movement."* According to *Merriam-Webster's Dictionary*, *dazzle* means, "to impress deeply, overpower, or confound with brilliance; to overpower with light; to lose clear vision especially from looking at bright light."

The dazzling, however, was not with the Lord. The dazzling had entered the prophetic movement regarding fame, influence, and even the exaltation of revelation. The Lord has been convicting and continually exposing many prophets and calling them to repentance, and they have not repented. This place of pride in the hearts of the prophets has opened the door for a spirit of perversion to come into the Church. Prophetic half-truths are being released, but they aren't being released from the heart of God. This demonic spirit is releasing prophetic words in order to manipulate, control, and blind. That is why in these days we must be asking for discernment.

There is going to be an exposing of false prophets in this new era. That is not an invitation for the body of Christ to go on a "false prophet" hunt, tearing down all the prophets and moving in accusation. This is going to be an exposing that will take place by the hand of God in order to protect His sheep.

I believe the Lord is calling the Church to a greater level of discernment and biblical knowledge in this new era in the prophetic. It's not the place of suspicion; it's the place of living so close to Jesus that you know His voice, you know the voice of the Holy Spirit, and you know the voice of the Father so well. When you hear a voice that is foreign to the One that you know and see in Scripture, you will recognize it (see 1 John 4:1; Heb. 5:14; 2 Pet. 2:1-22).

The Lord continued to speak:

> "It's not about prophetic words. It's not about platforms. It's not about numbers. It's not about your ministry or your name; it is about living in the place of deep intimacy with Me where you are My friend and I can trust you with My heart and My secrets."

I was then undone by His words: *"I am looking for the prophets whom I can trust with My heart."*

The fire of God coming upon the prophetic movement will offend the minds of those who don't have eyes to see and ears to hear. The purging and rearranging of the hand of the Lord will bring offense to the religious mindset and places of pride. Those with clean hands and pure hearts will embrace the rearranging of the Lord and partner with His realignment and reshaping of the prophetic movement (see Ps. 24:4).

In this fire and purging that's coming, the Lord is bringing down the worship of self, of the prophetic, and of prophetic words. He is bringing us back to the true, pure worship of Jesus. In some ways among prophets and the body of Christ, the prophetic has become an "idol" to worship. The fire of God is coming down upon that place to bring a proper balance—the plumb line to the prophetic movement. It's not a place of not needing the prophetic at all, but neither is it the worship of prophetic words and who has the best word or latest revelation.

It Is Time for My Prophets to Be Discipled

The Lord continued to speak: *"It's time for My prophets to be discipled."* I noticed this time the Lord did not say "many." He spoke generally of *all prophets.* I instantly thought of the vision of the twelve standing in the line that I shared previously. I heard His whisper:

"As we have entered this new era, there are new things that I want to teach My prophets. There are new ways of prophesying and bringing forth My government upon the earth through the clarity of My divine strategy that I want to release to them. It's the invitation into Jeremiah 33:3. The issue for many prophets is they think they understand completely and they know it all. They are walking in a form of pride that I abhor. I am inviting My prophets in this new era into a realm of understanding My Spirit of wisdom and revelation and the secrets of My heart—things they do not yet know. The place of Daniel 2:22, where I reveal deep and mysterious things and what is hidden in darkness, and if there is pride in the heart My prophets cannot enter this place. It takes humility to enter into this new realm of wisdom and revelation from My Word that I want to release to My prophets, which will be then released as My rhema word like fire in their mouths to bring needed reformation and maturing. It's a new time when I want to disciple My prophets in the new thing that I am doing."

A strong sense surrounded me of the foundation of Scripture. The Lord was inviting His prophets into deeper levels of encounter with Him in the Word where He was going to unlock deeper treasures and mysteries that are needed for this new era. In the spirit I could hear the sound of a hammer and a gavel coming down at the same time. The Lord is inviting the prophets into a deeper realm of being discipled by His Spirit to see the Word of the Lord released through their mouths like a hammer to bring down strongholds, and to see the divine justice of God executed upon the earth. Humility was the key—recognizing that we know and prophesy in part (see 1 Cor. 13:9). The Lord will have prophets release words in this new era that will call His people to account and bring correction in love to position the Church to run with God like never before. Some of these prophetic words will not be "loved" by many because they will call out biblical truths of laying down your life and following Jesus, repenting of the idols, and calling the people of God back to their first love. They will call God's people into a new realm of walking in holiness and the fear of God.

The Lord showed me that He wants to release His heart for His Church to the prophets in this discipling. The tone of the Lord has changed, and the prophetic words are being sent forth into the body of Christ. It reminded me of when I was at Glory City Church in 2019 and heard David Wagner speak. He said, "Some prophets just need to fall in love with the Church again."

Part of the discipling that I saw God bringing in this new era was that very thing. God wants to release His heart for the Church to His prophets in deeper ways. Prophetic words should not be released out of judgment, frustration, or offense but out of the heart of the Father, for the love of His people, to bring them into alignment and call them to prepare themselves as a pure and spotless Bride.

There will also be a discipling that the Lord will bring to the prophets who are called to the seven mountains of influence—government, education, business, family, media, finance, and the arts. The Lord is going to disciple and teach the prophets with mandates in these mountains of influence the strategies that He is downloading and the blueprints He is releasing to see people come to know Jesus, extend the Kingdom of God, and impact cities by the goodness and love of Jesus. The Lord is going to begin to disciple His prophets in translating the prophetic for the kings of the earth on a scale we have never seen, because this is the day for the Josephs and Daniels to arise.

I Saw the Shofars Sounding

The encounter continued, and I was lifted above the body of Christ and I saw many shofars being sounded. I knew instantly that they represented the prophets releasing prophetic words. There were many different sounds, shapes, and sizes of shofars. I noticed that the shofars were connected to "wells." The wells were where the prophets received the revelation, and then the sound was released from the shofars. I then heard the Lord say: *"Look beyond the surface."*

Instantly, it was like my eyes were sharpened in the spirit and I saw water beneath the surface of these wells. The top layer of the water looked normal, but as I looked deeper the waters were contaminated. His voice surrounded me again:

> "The waters are being muddied. The waters are being contaminated by many things. The waters are being muddied by self-promotion. The waters are being muddied by compromise and fear of man. The waters are being muddied by words being released that are not coming from a place of deep intimacy but a place of *manufacture*. The waters are being muddied by sin."

The Lord wasn't saying that all prophets are prophesying from impure wells, but He was highlighting that the prophetic stream was being contaminated by these issues in the prophetic movement. The Lord then spoke again:

> "There are many prophetic words that are being released in the body of Christ right now that are not from My heart and are being released to create platform and influence. 'Simon the sorcerers' are arising in the Church, and I am inviting My prophets back to the table of intimacy with Me again to allow Me to examine their hearts in the light of My presence and My fire to purify and prepare them for what is to come and what they are to carry in this new era."

Simon the sorcerers! My goodness! That took me by surprise! I was totally shocked and stunned. Let's look at Acts 8:9-23:

> *A man named Simon had been a sorcerer there for many years, amazing the people of Samaria and claiming to be someone great. Everyone, from the least to the greatest, often spoke of him as "the Great One—the Power of God." They listened closely to him because for a long time he had astounded them with his magic.*
>
> *But now the people believed Philip's message of Good News concerning the Kingdom of God and the name of Jesus Christ. As a result, many men and women were baptized. Then Simon himself believed and was baptized. He began following Philip wherever he went, and he was amazed by the signs and great miracles Philip performed.*
>
> *When the apostles in Jerusalem heard that the people of Samaria had accepted God's message, they sent Peter and John there. As soon as they arrived, they prayed for these new believers to receive the Holy Spirit. The Holy Spirit had not yet come upon any of them, for they had only been baptized in the name of the Lord Jesus. Then Peter and John laid their hands upon these believers, and they received the Holy Spirit.*
>
> *When Simon saw that the Spirit was given when the apostles laid their hands on people, he offered them money to buy this power. "Let me have this power, too," he exclaimed, "so that when I lay my hands on people, they will receive the Holy Spirit!"*
>
> *But Peter replied, "May your money be destroyed with you for thinking God's gift can be bought! You can have no part*

in this, for your heart is not right with God. Repent of your wickedness and pray to the Lord. Perhaps he will forgive your evil thoughts, for I can see that you are full of bitter jealousy and are held captive by sin" (NLT).

The key the Lord spoke to me from that passage was that *Simon wanted the power.* Now, there is nothing wrong with wanting to move in the power of God. Jesus said that signs and wonders would follow those who believe (see Mark 16:17-18), but it was Simon's heart that was the issue. As Peter said to him in verses 20-23:

> *May your money be destroyed with you for thinking God's gift can be bought! You can have no part in this, for your heart is not right with God. Repent of your wickedness and pray to the Lord. Perhaps he will forgive your evil thoughts, for I can see that you are full of bitter jealousy and are held captive by sin* (NLT).

Here was the place of wanting to move in the power of God but without relationship. His motivation was jealousy and he was in sin. It was a form of spiritual prostitution.

When speaking with a friend recently, I mentioned this revelation to her that the Lord had spoken to me about Simon the sorcerer. She mentioned that Jeremiah Johnson had also heard the same thing from the Lord. I came across this quote in his book *Cleansing and Igniting the Prophetic: An Urgent Wake-Up Call,* and it articulates so well what I believe the Lord is speaking from Acts 8.

> There is a divine confrontation quickly approaching the contemporary prophetic movement. I see a collision between a breed of Simon the Sorcerers who are going to be exposed for the illegitimate authority that they walk

in and an ignited and purified company of prophets and prophetic people who walk in true kingdom authority birthed out of intimacy. Beware of these Simon the Sorcerers. They are addicted to ministry and crave the power and anointing of God from an impure heart of jealousy and a selfish desire to be famous. Instead of carrying a living and active spirit of revelation, Simon the Sorcerer types have to borrow revelation because they have no prayer life. Simon told Peter and John in Acts 8:24, "Pray to the Lord for me yourselves, so that nothing of what you have said may come upon me." The greatest distinction between this breed of Simon the Sorcerers and the ignited and cleansed prophetic voices will be deep intimacy with Jesus that can only be birthed through deep intercession and travail. Simon the Sorcerers are looking to get launched into ministry by another's touch, but the ignited and cleansed prophetic generation is looking to grow in humility under heaven's touch. This can only be accomplished through prayer and fasting.[3]

There is a very clear distinction and divine separating that is coming to the prophetic movement by the hand of the Lord, releasing His fire to purify. The days of seeing the prophetic in operation in the Church and the earth in *power* are upon us in this new era; it's closer than we may think.

Don't Rush on the Release of Prophetic Words

Let's go back to the encounter. As I continued to seek His heart, I heard the Lord say:

"In this new era My prophets do *not rush* on the release of prophetic words. The mysteries and the secrets I will release to you and through you will bring transformation and reformation unlike anything you have ever seen as you live from the pure well of deep intimacy with Me and heart health before Me—the positioning of humility and integrity. It is imperative in this new era of *rapid acceleration* that you, My prophets, are living in deeper *communication* and *saturation*. It's time to *linger* more than you have ever lingered. Do not get caught up in the acceleration where the ministry and opportunity outweigh the place of intimacy and saturation in My presence and My Word.

"*Marination and maturation* is *crucial* in this new era. Allow the words I speak to you to *marinate*, to *mature*, and continue to ask for discernment and wisdom from Me to guide you in the timing and release of when and what to share (see James 1:5). For I will add layers of revelation upon words I am releasing in this new era that you will miss if you release them too quickly."

The Lord is summoning His prophets deeper into the Word. In preparation for what is coming, the Lord is calling the prophets to invest more time *in the Word* than releasing the words. The Lord is calling the prophets to a deeper place of *marinating* in the Word and a greater *maturing* will take place within them.

Minister to Him First

The Lord showed me where ministry and the release of prophetic words has become an idol and the focus upon building a platform and having influence has become the main thing in the lives of many prophets. I then heard the Lord say:

> **"The prophets who will continue to arise with the pure words of My heart in this new era will be those who minister to Me first, before ministry to the saints."**

The invitation to minister to the Lord first is going to weigh heavier and heavier on the prophets in this new era. The place of deep consecration to the Lord is going to weigh heavier than ever, and these prophets will be the ones who will continue to arise with the pure word of the Lord, bringing the plumb line, alignment, transformation, and reformation in the areas the Lord releases them into. The Lord spoke again:

> **"These prophets will *obey* and release the words I am releasing without compromise, without apology, and will speak My words without watering them down or adapting them to tickle ears. They will speak with boldness, unhindered by the fear of man, releasing the word of the Lord with purity, with an accurate depiction of My heart and My nature, not bowing to the expectations of man but speaking forth My words."**

There's a call from the heart of God to the prophets to draw closer to Him than ever before. To allow Him to examine hearts in the light of His presence. There is a repentance that the Lord is calling for. Allow the fire of God to come and burn away all that needs to be burned away—areas of compromise, areas of mixture, areas of pride, areas of self-promotion, areas of manipulation and misuse of the prophetic gifting and operating in witchcraft. This is to prepare the prophets to carry the pure words of the Lord for this new era. Copying prophetic words, jealousy among many prophets, prostitution of His voice—it must stop.

This confrontation, this alignment, this move of His hand and the refiner's fire will bring forth such an awakening to the privilege that it is to hear His voice. Many prophets will fall in repentance, and others will run in the opposite direction. There cannot be a mucking around and playing games with the voice of the Lord anymore. I heard the Lord speaking strongly: *"Do you not realize who speaks to you?"*

A mighty wave of travail is going to come over the prophetic movement. There will be a mighty, repentant cry that will arise as the conviction of the Holy Spirit falls. Those with humility and intimacy will see it and recognize it and intercede for those who are caught in pride, rebellion, and spiritual prostitution. Those who are friends of God, living close to His heart, will not use this time to throw stones at other prophets, judge, and condemn, but they will stand in intercession, crying out to the Lord to forgive the prophets for any misuse of His voice.

Prophets of His heart, as the grief on the Lord's heart falls upon you in intercession—do not fight it; embrace it. Embrace the longings and the cry of His heart, because in your intercession there will be great alignment that will take place. Guard your heart by staying close to His, receiving His heart of love for those who are moving in impurity. Partner with the Lord in His strategies of prayer, intercession, and the delivery of the prophetic word to see the structures in the prophetic movement that were built by man, not established by the Lord, be dismantled in this new era.

It's time for us to see the prophetic operate in power in a way we have never seen. To see not only prophetic words released from the Lord received in power, but the strategies and wisdom of God in place to build with Him in this new era to see transformation in the earth in accelerated ways.

We must embrace the fire that's upon the prophetic movement to prepare us to see the prophetic build with God in the earth on a scale we have never seen. Let the prophets come before the Lord and cry out:

> *God, I invite your searching gaze into my heart. Examine me through and through; find out everything that may be hidden within me. Put me to the test and sift through all my anxious cares. See if there is any path of pain I'm walking on, and lead me back to your glorious, everlasting ways—the path that brings me back to you* (Psalm 139:23-24 TPT).

My heart is that in all that God does in this new era—in His new tone, in the correction, in the place where the Church has been weighed and found wanting—we will see His heart of *love* to get our attention and to bring us into right alignment to partner with Him in the greatest move of the Spirit of God in the earth that we have ever seen.

Let our continual prayer in this new era be, "Lord, show me *how* to be ready."

> *Let us rejoice and exult and give him the glory, for the marriage of the Lamb has come, and his Bride has made herself ready* (Revelation 19:7 ESV).

> *Search me, O God, and know my heart; test me and know my anxious thoughts. Point out anything in me that offends*

you, and lead me along the path of everlasting life (Psalm 139:23-24 NLT).

Notes

1. Adam F. Thompson and Adrian Beale, *The Divinity Code* (Shippensburg, PA: Destiny Image Publishers, 2011), 560.

2. Lexico, powered by Oxford, s.v. "plumb line," https://www.lexico.com/definition/plumb_line.

3. Jeremiah Johnson, *Cleansing and Igniting the Prophetic: An Urgent Wake-Up Call* (Shippensburg, PA: Destiny Image Publishers, 2018), 98.

Chapter Thirteen

THIS BOOK IS AN INVITATION

My assignment from the Lord in writing this book was one thing—to release the keys that He has given me for this new era. Are they all the keys? No, but I believe that they are foundational keys for what the Lord is going to do in this new era.

These keys have been given to you from the heart of God to prepare you, to align you, to position you for what is going to be the greatest revealing of His glory and the majesty of Jesus Christ that we have ever seen. This is the time of Habakkuk 2:14: *"For as the waters fill the sea, the earth will be filled with an awareness of the glory of the Lord"* (NLT).

The greatest days of the Church are upon us—the days of being reintroduced to His power and the Church walking in all that Jesus purchased at Calvary. It is the great awakening to the love of God and the nature of God. The awakening to sonship in greater ways and the awakening to the authority we carry in Christ. It's the invitation to know the ways of God, for His ways are not our ways and His thoughts are not our thoughts (see Isa. 55:8-9).

This book is a line in the sand. It's an invitation to make a decision to follow Him. It's the invitation into the greatest adventure you have walked thus far with Jesus. It's the hour to understand that when we lose our life, we will find it in Him. God is leading us further into the abundant life of John 10:10. It is because of the extravagant love of such a good Father that He is preparing us to carry what He is going to release. As Bill Johnson says, "God corrects and disciplines so His blessings don't kill us." God is preparing us in so many ways for what is to come. He is inviting us into that place of a fresh *yes* to Him. If it doesn't look the way we expect or come when we expect, we are okay with that because we live in the yielded place, completely and totally in love with Jesus here on earth so that our lives may be used to bring Him glory.

He's coming in power!

It's time for you to step into your destiny and run with Him like you have never run before. It is time for you to see the Lord move through you in ways you never thought possible. It's time for you to step into the greater realms of joy of knowing Him and making Him known on the earth.

It's time for the Church to move deeper into maturity as sons and daughters of God, recognizing the times and the seasons, being led by His wisdom, knowing His ways, and building with Him.

What exciting days we live in! We are going to see the impossible become possible. This is the hour of Esther 4:14:

> *For if you keep silent at this time, relief and deliverance will rise for the Jews from another place, but you and your father's house will perish. And who knows whether you have not come to the kingdom for such a time as this?* (ESV)

The *kairos* season! The appointed time! Fullness is upon us!

> *So wake up, you living gateways! Lift up your heads, you ageless doors of destiny! Welcome the King of Glory, for he is about to come through you. You ask, "Who is this Glory-King?" The Lord, armed and ready for battle, the Mighty One, invincible in every way! So wake up, you living gateways, and rejoice! Fling wide, you ageless doors of destiny! Here he comes; the King of Glory is ready to come in* (Psalm 24:7-9 TPT).

> *Let us rejoice and exult and give him the glory, for the marriage of the Lamb has come, and his Bride has made herself ready* (Revelation 19:7 ESV).

I implore you to keep seeking His heart. Embrace the fire and moving of the Holy Spirit in your life. It's the call to be *all in*. Nothing held back. All of you. The era of the unexpected is upon us! The decade of deliverance has arrived! The era to walk in His wisdom and His ways and see transformation and reformation in unprecedented ways.

He is calling us into our responsibility as the Bride to ready ourselves.

"Make room! Get ready! I'm coming...ready or not!"

ABOUT LANA VAWSER

Lana Vawser is, first and foremost, a pursuer of God's heart and, second, a prophetic voice to the nations. Her desire is to help people develop deep intimacy with Jesus and activate their prophetic hearing to recognize God speaking in everyday life. Lana is driven by a vision to see people set free and walking in the abundant life that Jesus purchased for them. She is an itinerant preacher and prophetic revivalist who gets to participate in powerful moves of God throughout the nations. Lana is married to Kevin and they live in Adelaide, South Australia with their three sons.

Made in the USA
Columbia, SC
12 September 2020